Folding Knives

The Complete Guide to Modern Pocketknives

Thomas Laible

4880 Lower Valley Road • Atglen, PA 19310

Copyright © 2025 by Schiffer Publishing, Ltd.

Originally published as *Folder* by Wieland Verlag, GmbH, Bad Aibling ©2023
Translated from the German by Catherine Venner

Library of Congress Control Number: 2024941294

All rights reserved. No part of this work may be reproduced or used in any form or by any means—graphic, electronic, or mechanical, including photocopying or information storage and retrieval systems—without written permission from the publisher.

The scanning, uploading, and distribution of this book or any part thereof via the Internet or any other means without the permission of the publisher is illegal and punishable by law. Please purchase only authorized editions and do not participate in or encourage the electronic piracy of copyrighted materials.

"Schiffer," "Schiffer Publishing, Ltd.," and the pen and inkwell logo are registered trademarks of Schiffer Publishing, Ltd.

Cover design by Jack Chappell
Type set in Alibaba Sans/Calluna

ISBN: 978-0-7643-6929-2
ePub: 978-1-5073-0554-6
Printed in India

Published by Schiffer Publishing, Ltd.
4880 Lower Valley Road
Atglen, PA 19310
Phone: (610) 593-1777; Fax: (610) 593-2002
Email: Info@schifferbooks.com
Web: www.schifferbooks.com

For our complete selection of fine books on this and related subjects, please visit our website at www.schifferbooks.com. You may also write for a free catalog.

Schiffer Publishing's titles are available at special discounts for bulk purchases for sales promotions or premiums. Special editions, including personalized covers, corporate imprints, and excerpts, can be created in large quantities for special needs. For more information, contact the publisher.

We are always looking for people to write books on new and related subjects. If you have an idea for a book, please contact us at proposals@schifferbooks.com.

Other Schiffer Books by the Author:
The Sword, ISBN 978-0-7643-4877-8

Other Schiffer Books on Related Subjects:
The Big Book of Knives: Everything about Mankind's Most Important Tool, Oliver Lang, ISBN 978-0-7643-5739-8
The Puukko: Finnish Knives from Antiquity to Today, Anssi Ruusuvuori, ISBN 978-0-7643-6070-1

NOTE: Check the laws and regulations in your location for proper owning and carrying of various folding knives.

Photo: Sharp by Coop

CONTENTS

PREFACE — 6

1 | PRACTICAL FOLDING KNIVES: WHAT ARE THEY? — 8
- Tactical Is Practical — 9
- Everyday Carry — 16
- Modern Practical Folding Knives — 19

2 | FROM TACTICAL TO PRACTICAL: THE EVOLUTION — 22
- Bob Terzuola and the ATCF — 25
- Technical Developments — 30
- Production in the Far East — 35

3 | SCIENCE AND ART: THE DESIGN — 42
- Key Questions — 45
- Functional Interplay — 52
- Affordable Quality — 57

4 | THE HANDLE: THE CONNECTION BETWEEN MAN AND KNIFE — 64
- The Handle Design — 65
- The Handle Construction — 70
- The Handle Materials — 77

5 | EDGY SHAPES: THE BLADES — 92
- The Blade Shapes — 93
- The Edge Geometry — 98
- The Grind Types — 106
- The Ideal Blade Length — 111

6 | FOR SAFETY'S SAKE: LOCKING SYSTEMS — 116
- The Liner Lock — 119
- The Frame Lock — 129
- The Back Lock — 137
- The Tri-Ad Lock — 139
- Axis Lock & Co. — 143
- Other Locking Systems — 145

7 | WITH ONE HAND: OPENING MECHANISMS — 152
- Blade Washers — 154
- Blade Motion — 159
- Blade Lifter — 161
- The Flipper — 166
- Switchblades and Assisted Openers — 173

8 | ALWAYS WITH YOU: THE CLIP — 178
- Left or Right, Tip Down or Tip Up? — 182
- Deep Carry and Rear Mounting — 185
- Types of Clips — 186
- Special Designs — 190

9 | LAWFUL WORK-AROUNDS: TWO-HANDED KNIVES AND SLIP JOINTS — 194
- Unscrewing the Blade Lifter — 198
- Modern Slip Joints — 201

10 | TECHNOLOGY AND PHILOSOPHY: THE TYPES OF STEEL — 206
- Stainless Steel — 214
- Powder Steel — 216
- Damascus Steel — 218
- Coatings and Finishings — 220
- Types of Steel and Their Properties — 222

11 | POLITICS AND KNIFE BANS — 226
- Background of Knife Bans — 227
- One-Handed Knives as the Enemy — 228
- Terror Attacks and Knife Bans — 232

APPENDIX — 236
- Index of Key Words — 236
- Knife Law — 238

PREFACE

Over the past twenty years, the knife sector has rapidly changed primarily because new technologies and production techniques have made new methods of construction and knife shapes possible. A look at the current range on the market shows that a large portion of pocketknives have features that in the 1990s would have still been regarded as markedly "tactical." These features most notably include one-handed operation, ergonomic handles, and pocket clips, but also materials such as micarta, G-10, titanium, carbon fiber, and powder steel. However, most modern pocketknives don't look tactical. And many users don't even regard them as tactical but rather as practical knives and useful companions in daily life.

So what exactly is the difference between tactical and practical? It's mainly the appearance: upon analyzing the construction and design of modern pocketknives, the real difference between practical and tactical functions can only rarely—or not at all—be discerned. That's because in many respects, tactical is simply practical.

So you could say that it's not actually a tactical folding knife but rather a practical folding knife.

This book intends to share more than just technical knowledge about practical folding knives, but also the philosophy behind them. Opponents of knife carrying could, of course, claim that this is a plea by a staunch knife nut in an attempt to sugarcoat a weapon by calling it a tool. But in fact, even the legislators register that there are similarities between tactical and practical. The German administrative provision to the German Weapons Act (Verwaltungsvorschrift zum Waffengesetz—WaffVwV) expressly emphasizes that modern one-handed knives "may be useful utility knives" and "are not essentially the same as weapons."

Therefore, practical folding knives are not military-tactical knives but, rather, utility pocketknives that feature modern technology and materials. This book shall answer all important questions on this topic. The following pages will examine the history of folding knives, locking mechanism, methods of construction, blade shapes, types of steel, and handle materials, as well as legal matters.

This book would not have been possible without the help of many people. First and foremost, my friend

Hadie Sievert, who not only allowed me to photograph valuable knives from his collection but supported the development of this book throughout with his constructive criticism. I would also like to thank the many companies who have provided me with sample products over the years. The beautiful photos and explanatory graphics came above all from Benchmade, Böhler, Böker, Buck, Cold Steel, CRKT, Fox Gerber, Kershaw, Pohl Force, Real Steel, Spyderco, and Victorinox. I received wonderful images from photography specialist Sharp by Coop as well as from my fellow authors Oliver Lang, Peter Fronteddu, Wolfgang Peter-Michel, Stefan Steigerwald, and H.J. Wieland. Last but not least, I would like to thank the team at Wieland Verlag for their patience during this project.

In addition to sharing knowledge, this book also intends to show the beauty of modern pocketknives and to awaken enthusiasm for them. I wish you all happy reading.

—*Thomas Laible*

The legendary ATCF design by Bob Terzuola sets the standard for modern folding knives.

Photo: Sharp by Coop

CHAPTER 1

PRACTICAL FOLDING KNIVES: WHAT ARE THEY?

A useful companion in daily life is exactly what a practical folding knife should be. They are extremely versatile cutting tools that, if possible, you should always and everywhere have on you. They are pocketknives that can be comfortably and easily worn thanks to a clip.

An important element of modern folding knives is one-handed handling. It needs no explanation how much more practical it makes a knife; it's not just about being able to quickly and easily open it, but also that you have your other hand free in order to hold what you are cutting. Once you've finished working, the knife can be closed again with just one hand and safely stored in your trouser pocket.

The danger of putting an open knife down and then later accidentally grabbing it by the blade and injuring yourself is reduced thanks to one-handed handling. Thus, it's no surprise that since they emerged in the 1980s, they have become the most important design on the market. That is clear from just glancing at the relevant catalogs and online shops.

"Be prepared!"
–Boy Scouts' motto–

TACTICAL IS PRACTICAL

In many respects, modern practical folding knives have developed from the tactical folding knives of the 1980s and 1990s, just as the universally loved Swiss Army Knife grew out of the original soldier's knife from 1891. For this reason, it's internationally known as the "Swiss Army Knife" and not the "Swiss Pocketknife." In the same way that the trench coat, originally an item worn in the military, became civilian clothing and GPS was developed from a US army navigation system into the basis of "satnavs" around the world, the modern practical pocketknife has its origins in the tactical pocketknife.

If you look at the basic features, it's hard to spot a difference between the

Opposite: The designs by well-known knife makers are pioneering examples for the industry. The elegant Q36 by RJ Martin was serial-produced for many years by Kershaw.

1 | PRACTICAL FOLDING KNIVES: WHAT ARE THEY?

Thanks to computer-controlled manufacturing, an almost endless variety of shapes and materials are available today. (Real Steel Megalodon · Giant Mouse ACE Biblio · Benchmade Gravitator)

practical and tactical folding knife. The only real difference is the appearance of the respective knife.

Although the term "tactical" has a military background, its meaning covers much more. According to the dictionary, tactic is a "determined manner of procedure in regard to expedience and success." Upon that basis the following definition can be derived: a tactical knife is a specially conceived knife for functionality and successful deployment.

At first it sounds like a platitude, but it's not. It's precisely seemingly simple designs that often require so many considerations about the functionality. From this point, it's just a small step to the practical folding knife. The specially conceived details, which were designed for military use, are also useful in civilian daily life. The definition of a specially designed knife applies to both tactical folding knives and also practical folding knives.

	PRACTICAL	TACTICAL
Pocket clip	•	•
Locking mechanism	•	•
One-handed handling	•	•
Ergonomic handle	•	•
Modern material	•	•
Tactical appearance	–	•

10

PRACTICAL FOLDING KNIVES: WHAT ARE THEY? | **1**

TRUE STORIES—KNIVES AS LIFESAVERS

Some people believe that you only need a knife at home or to do work that has been planned in advance, so they ask, Why would you need a knife in your pocket? The thrust of their argument is "I'm not going on a survival tour, so why would I need a knife?" Yet, surely everybody has, at some time, been in a situation where they needed a knife but didn't have one with them. If only I had a dollar for every time somebody borrowed my pocketknife . . .

I also wish I'd started to file all those stories in which a knife turns into a lifesaving tool. Fortunately, Swiss company Victorinox has collected many of these stories under the heading "True Stories." The Swiss Army Knife is the most popular pocketknife in the world. It's therefore no surprise that this knife played a starring role in many of these lifesaving stories. Many grateful knife owners have written to the manufacturer Victorinox and told their story. A selection of these stories has been collated and published at **www.victorianox.com**.

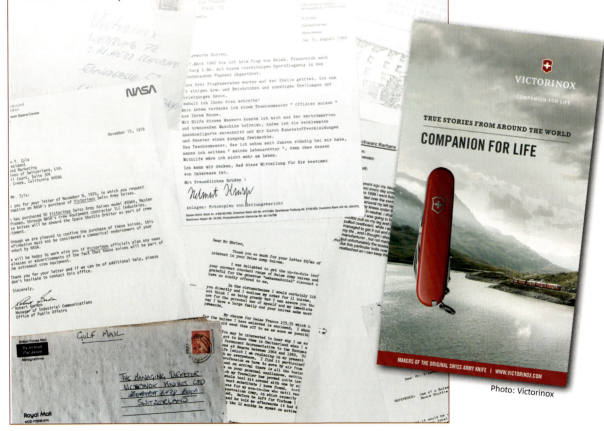

Photo: Victorinox

1 | PRACTICAL FOLDING KNIVES: WHAT ARE THEY?

WHAT IS WHAT?

❶ Blade

❷ Blade lifter: for one-handed opening using your thumb—in the form of a thumb stud, thumb disk, or thumb hole

❸ Flipper: used both for one-handed opening as well as hand protection when the blade is folded out

❹ Pivot pin

❺ Liner: form the handle frame and are made of either steel or titanium

❻ Handle scales: aid slip resistance and better hand positioning and are screwed to the liner

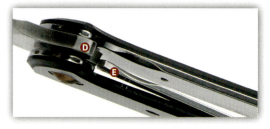

Ⓐ **Clip:** to attach the knife to a trouser pocket

Ⓑ **Lanyard hole:** (safety strap ring): to attach the knife to a hand strap or toggle

Ⓒ **Backspacer:** spacer between the liners—it may take various shapes

Ⓓ **Tang:** the part of the blade that is farthest back and hidden in the handle.

Ⓔ **Locking system:** in this example, a tried-and-tested liner lock

Ⓕ **Flipper (nose):** when the blade is folded, it generally protrudes just out of the back of the handle

Photos: CRKT

PRACTICAL FOLDING KNIVES: WHAT ARE THEY?

You can explain the usefulness of a pocketknife in general and of a practical folding knife in particular in more detail by way of a few theories:

Theory 1: A knife is a useful tool. Almost everybody owns one and uses it regularly.

Theory 2: A knife can only be useful as a tool when it's at hand. You need to have it with you to be able to use it in unforeseeable situations. There is nothing more useless than a pocketknife at home in a drawer, if you need one when you are out.

Theory 3: In the case of accidents and emergency situations, it's not enough to have a knife in your backpack or your bag. It must be within easy reach to be able to use it.

Theory 4: In the worst-case scenario, a lack of a knife could be life-threatening.

There is surely just a handful of people who do not own even one knife, and in reality, nobody would contradict theory 1. However, it's different for theory 2. In fact, there are a lot of people who do not regularly carry a knife. The majority of people in the industrialized West keep their knives in kitchen drawers, in a cupboard, or in a toolbox.

Thanks to one-handed operation, it has become considerably easier to use a pocketknife. (Real Steel H6 *Elegance*)

1 | PRACTICAL FOLDING KNIVES: WHAT ARE THEY?

Photos: CRKT

Whether they are traditionally handcrafted or created with modern production methods, knives are an essential tool and have been used by humans for thousands of years. (CRKT M16)

Yet, almost everyone has been in a situation where they have needed a knife but didn't have one with them. There are also numerous reports of incidents in which a knife became a lifesaving tool (see info box, page 11). The "True Stories" collected by Victorinox are good evidence for theories 3 and 4.

A Swiss Army Knife saved the life of a driver. The thirty-eight-year-old was on a federal highway close to Oldendorf, when he lost control of his vehicle while overtaking. The car skidded over the opposite lane, grazed a tree, turned over in the ditch, ended up on its roof, and caught fire. The badly injured driver was hanging upside down in his safety belt.

The people who'd rushed to help couldn't release the belt. Fortunately, among them was seventy-three-year-old pensioner Rüdiger L., who always carries a Swiss Army Knife from Victorinox with him. Risking his own life, he cut through the belt, literally at the very last minute, since the driver's trousers and jacket were already burning.

Such car accidents are a daily occurrence. According to figures from the German Federal Statistical Office, in the year 2020 there were 264,423 accidents involving injury to persons, and 2,719 people were killed. That amounts to 732 accidents resulting in injury and seven deaths each day. Those who can reach for a sharp knife in case of an accident are safer.

The international success of the multifunctional Swiss Army Knife appears to validate those people who dispute the advantages of all modern pocketknives with locking systems and one-handed operation. They only consider such knives to be weapons and therefore are in favor of restriction. Of course, you can still cut something with a traditional pocketknife, but in comparison, modern practical folding knives offer functional advantages.

The call for tender for the current pocketknife for the Swiss Army summarizes the technical developments. "The old soldiers' knife no longer corresponds to today's requirements in terms of safety and technology," the procurement office of the Swiss Army, Armasuisse, explained. "For example, the blade is not lockable, meaning that when used, it may cause injuries."

The awareness that a pocketknife may be a lifesaver in daily life was one of the determining factors in the development of the modern practical folding knife. Therefore, theory 3 brings us back to the term "pocketknife." A pocketknife, as the name already suggests, is intended to be carried daily in the pockets of your clothes. The modern expression for this philosophy is the term "*Every Day Carry—EDC.*"

THE GINGERBREAD HOUSE

I attended a very Catholic secondary school, where I assume more attention was paid to correct manners than would be at a normal public school. At a class Christmas party—it must have been in 1983 or 1984—one of the other pupils brought in a homemade, and unfortunately very hard, gingerbread house. My class teacher found an easy solution to the problem, saying, "Thomas, most likely you have your knife with you. Bring it over; we need it now!" A pocketknife at school, back then peacefully used as a cake cutter. Nowadays, it would probably cause the police to be called, followed by psychological support for the "traumatized pupils" and disciplinary action against the knife owner.

Photo: Madeleine Steinbach/AdobeStock

Above: **The clip is the essential element of modern folding knives. It revolutionized how knives are carried in daily life. (CRKT Mah-Hawk)**

Opposite: **Even "tacticool" pocketknives are used primarily as useful aids for everyday work. (CRKT Drifter)**

EVERYDAY CARRY

Back in the day, "real boys" always had a pocketknife with them. For example, in Mark Twain's *Adventures of Tom Sawyer*, Tom, upon receiving his first knife, was swept away by a "convulsion of delight." If Tom Sawyer is too mundane for you, maybe take a look at the prince of poets, Johann Wolfgang von Goethe: in his memoires, Goethe describes how in his youth he used his "beautiful pocketknife" as a love oracle.

Even in the 1980s, pocketknives did not by any manner or means trigger any of the hysteria that today is linked to knives. Even former German Federal Chancellor Helmut Kohl (1930–2017) was a self-confessed knife carrier. He liked to give his friends in the Christian Democratic Union Party specially made pocketknives with his signature, and at party events he often organized a little snack: he would cut the sausage himself with his pocketknife and then pass the slice to his colleagues on the tip of his knife, as was reported by the German news magazine *Der Spiegel* in 1992.

Today, only a few people in public life admit to carrying a pocketknife. One of these few people is the famous musician Peter Maffay, who openly claims that as a "reminiscence of his childhood," he never leaves the house without a pocketknife. "That is a habit, in the same way as Bavarians wear their leather trousers," Maffay told the press. In answer to the question of why he still carries a knife with him today, he said, "You just never know."

PRACTICAL FOLDING KNIVES: WHAT ARE THEY? | 1

In the 1990s, many parents started to frown on items like pocketknives, and they were considered dangerous for children. TV increasingly spread the image that only criminal youth gangs had knives. Many people no longer thought of the trusty Swiss Army Knife but, rather, of scenes like James Dean's *Rebel without a Cause* (1955) or the knife fight in *West Side Story* (1961).

OLD SCHOOL OR MODERN

A sadly deceased friend and author colleague of mine was not a pronounced knife fan but regularly used his pocketknife. As a lover of traditionally handmade firearms, he also always preferred traditional hunting models of pocketknives, such as the Buck 110. After many of our conversations, he grew curious and decided to give a practical folding knife a try. After about a week, he called to tell me with enthusiasm that he couldn't have imagined how much more practical a one-handled knife with a clip is in daily life.

Photo: CRKT

1 | PRACTICAL FOLDING KNIVES: WHAT ARE THEY?

Whether a knife appears more tactical or more practical is often just a matter of color, as shown by these Real Steel Huginns, which are identical in terms of construction.

Innumerable episodes of TV crime dramas leave an impression that is both negative and incorrect. Unfortunately, these days many people associate pocketknives primarily with youth criminality and violence.

However, there are also positive examples in the media: in pop culture, carrying a knife, above all a Swiss Army Knife, has become known through *MacGyver* and later the TV show *NCIS*. The hit show follows the adventures of a unit in the prosecution arm of the US Navy (Naval Criminal Investigative Service). The head of the unit, Leroy Gibbs (Mark Harmon), goes through a series of consecutively numbered rules, which also rub off on his team and save their lives numerous times. Gibb's rule number 9 is "Never go anywhere without a knife!" Among knife enthusiasts it has become a familiar quote, and you frequently see "#9" patches on clothing or bags in support of this stance.

While some people do without pocketknives in their daily lives, as a result of the political developments in recent years, there are also many citizens who, undeterred, maintain the pocketknife culture and feel almost naked without a knife. Of course, that group includes knife enthusiasts who value quality craftmanship, sharp blades, and great design. In addition, there are also the EDC fans, who according to the old Scout's motto "Be prepared" always want to have something with them that will assist them in daily life and also potential emergencies.

MODERN PRACTICAL FOLDING KNIVES

Even if "old school" pocketknives are practical aids, the term "practical folding knife" refers to modern pocketknives with their integral features: ergonomic grip, one-handed operation, locking system, and clip. Traditional pocketknives continue to work reliably, and numerous owners are even today still completely satisfied with them. However, other users have different functionality requirements. Regarding the aspects of safety, portability, and handling comfort, modern practical folding knives are clearly superior. It's like vintage cars: no car lover would seriously question the practical use of airbags, power steering, central locking, air conditioning, and parking assistance.

However, compared to the traditional Swiss Army Knife, the majority of modern practical folding knives have one disadvantage: they are generally only equipped with one blade.

They generally don't have additional tools, such as bottle and tin openers. That does not appear to bother many users—with classic knives, such as Laguiole or Opinel, you also don't miss them, and at the end of the day, cutting is the main task of a knife. The manufacturers of Swiss Army Knives have recognized this need and are now selling lockable and one-handed knives in addition to the classic designs. And there are also always new modern one-handed knives, where additional tools are integrated in the handle.

All in all, safe locking mechanisms, comfortable one-handed operation, and, above all, the pocket clip are functional advantages that the majority of users now no longer want to do without. And that is how the tactical folding knife became the practical folding knife.

Photo: Leatherman

Some modern practical folding knives integrate multifunctional tools. (Leatherman Free K4)

1 | PRACTICAL FOLDING KNIVES: WHAT ARE THEY?

The vast diversity of modern pocketknives ensures a suitable model for all tastes and all budgets. (CRKT Terrestrial · Kizer Rattler · Tuya Bruiser · Spyderco Domino · WE Knife Bullit)

PRACTICAL FOLDING KNIVES: WHAT ARE THEY? | **1**

CHAPTER 2
FROM TACTICAL TO PRACTICAL: THE EVOLUTION

Even though modern practical folding knives are now regarded as utility knives, their roots go back to the tactical folding knives of the late 1980s. Some of the most important figures in their journey were Spyderco founder Sal Glesser and a few knife makers such as Bob Terzuola. In 1980, Spyderco developed a design for a completely new type of knife. For Sal Glesser and his wife, Gail, who until then had only manufactured and sold sharpeners, it was their very first knife. The Spyderco Worker was the first time that the three fundamental technical elements of today's conventional one-hand knives were brought together. These features are also the essential characteristics of practical folding knives:

- one-handed blade operation
- locking mechanism
- pocket clip

In the 1960s and 1970s, very popular pocketknives such as the widely distributed Buck 110 were designed for two-handed operation, and therefore the blade had a traditional nail notch.

To compensate for this drawback, resourceful nerds developed the Flick-it. This aid was a precursor to today's blade lifter and enabled the knife to be opened with one hand. The Flick-it was pushed onto the back of the blade on commercially available folding knives and then fixed in place with a screw.

However, for Spyderco boss Glesser, the Flick-it and similar constructions were not a good solution. After some experimenting, Sal finally came up with the idea of drilling a hole into the blade,

"Tradition is not worshiping the ashes, but sharing the flame."

–Jean Jaurès–

Opposite: **The Epicenter by knife maker Todd Rexford combines all functional elements of a modern practical folding knife with an elegant design.**

23

2 | FROM TACTICAL TO PRACTICAL: THE EVOLUTION

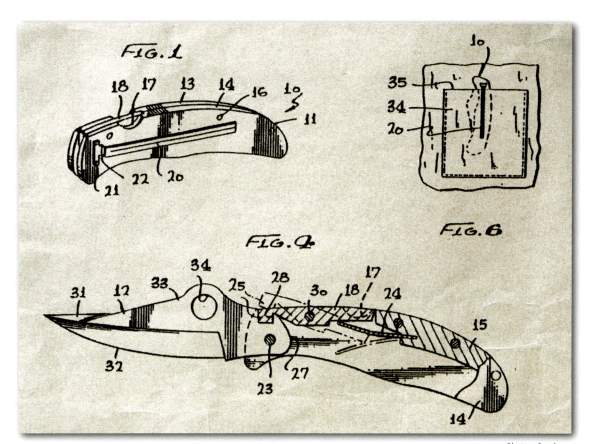

Photos: Spyderco

The Spyderco Worker was the very first modern one-handed knife and was patented in 1980.

which also enabled left-handed users to open it. The thumb hole is just one among the many blade lifters on the market (more on this later).

However, one of the other features invented by Sal Glesser has become established around the world and is now indispensable: the pocket clip. Until then, the only alternative to carrying a knife in your trouser pockets was a knife sheath on a belt. However, such holsters are considerably less practical than a trouser pocket—and they can't be worn in every situation without attracting attention and causing offense in social settings.

The clip revolutionized the way pocketknives are carried. Today, there is a clip on the vast majority of folding knives. Many classic knives have been reengineered—there is even a model of the legendary Buck 110 with a clip and blade lifter. Many customers no longer want to do without this very practical feature that has been tried and tested for over thirty years.

A further, important element in the evolution of the practical folding knife also originated in the early 1980s: US American knife maker Michael Walker improved the previously used spring locking system for pocketknives and made it globally popular, calling it the liner lock. Today the majority of pocketknives manufactured or hand-crafted use this system.

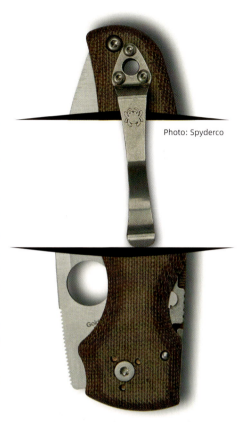

Photo: Spyderco

The clip on a pocketknife was a truly revolutionary idea. It changed the manner in which a knife could be carried, forever.

BOB TERZUOLA AND THE ATCF

While Sal Glesser from Spyderco invented the modern one-handed knife and did pioneering work, it was individual knife makers with their innovative designs who paved the way to the modern practical folding knife. The origins of many of these designs are found in tactical folding knives, whose evolution was shaped by several fundamental considerations:

1) The knife should be able to perform an array of cutting tasks with an effectiveness that is as consistent as possible.

2 | FROM TACTICAL TO PRACTICAL: THE EVOLUTION

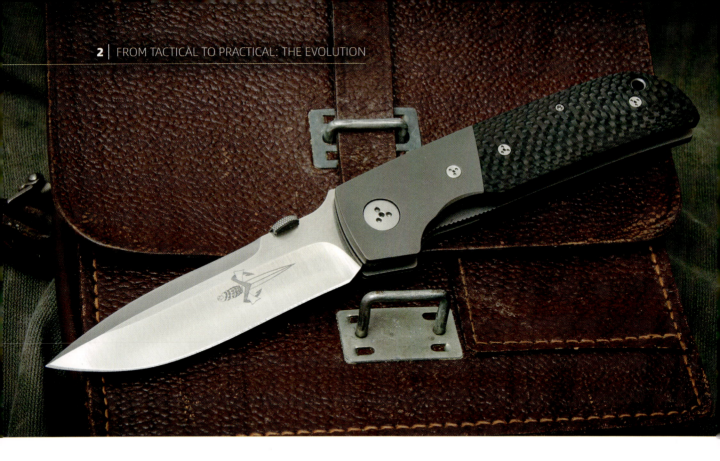

The legendary ATCF design is the ancestor of the modern tactical folding knife. The images show the very rare small series model by Microtech.

2) The knife should be as simply and easily accessible as possible both in daily life and for unexpected emergencies.
3) The knife should also be suitable as a means of defense in the case of an emergency.

While for the majority of knife enthusiasts, point 3 is no longer a criterion, points 1 and 2 continue to form the essence of a practical folding knife. Above all, American knife maker Robert "Bob" Terzuola was style-defining in this development. His legendary ATCF design is considered the ancestor of all tactical folding knives, and therefore, ultimately the father of the modern practical folding knife.

During the 1980s, Terzuola became increasingly aware that it's not just the military or the police who encounter emergency situations, but that they also happen in civilian day-to-day life. The best knife is absolutely useless if you don't have it when you need it. This recognition was Terzuola's starting point.

Bob designed a knife that you should always have on you; a knife that was comfortable to carry and easy to access and to open. It was intended as a versatile utility knife but also a lifesaver and a means of defense.

BUCK *110*: TRADITION VS. MODERN

The **110** Folding Hunter model by Buck takes its place among the great classic knives. Since the 1960s, it has been manufactured without interruption. The design inspired many other knife producers and has also been copied countless times. Although the **110** is still produced true to the original design, there are now also a variety of models with tactical design features, which are aimed at customers who prefer modern functions.

- The traditional **110** has a slim Bowie blade made of 420HC steel, which is folded out with two hands by using the nail notch and is locked with a back lock. The handle has a brass body with double bolster and handle inlays made of ebony. The 204-gram (7.2-ounce) knife is worn on a belt with a leather sheaf.
- The **110 Slim Pro** has the same profile, and the back lock is also positioned on the end of the handle in the old-fashioned way. The blade is made of 154CM steel and can be folded out with one hand by using the thumb pin on both sides. The handle is made of self-supporting micarta handle scales with additional liners, and as a result, it's clearly thinner. The 85g (3-ounce) knife is carried using the pocket clip, which can be converted for left-hand carry.

A classic Buck 110 and a modern Slim Pro model

Photos: Buck

2 | FROM TACTICAL TO PRACTICAL: THE EVOLUTION

At a time when large pocketknives were generally still carried in a belt sheath, Terzuola used a pocket clip, which in his opinion was the most practical and comfortable solution for carrying a pocketknife. Bob Terzuola was the first knife maker to use Spyderco's pocket clip invention on a handcrafted custom knife.

Size is an important factor for a pocketknife. As we will see in the chapter about blades, a longer blade allows for a more effective cut thanks to the dynamic edge angle. On the other hand, a larger folding knife can't be easily transported in trouser pockets, since the mechanics that need to be housed mean that the handle is noticeably longer than the blade. The conclusion: the knife should be as compact as necessary and as big as possible.

Another issue taken into account regarding size was weapons legislation. In many US states, the length of the blade is limited by the law to 4 inches (10.2 cm), 3.5 inches (8.9 cm), or sometimes even smaller. Therefore, Terzuola's designs have blades that are generally between 3.5 and just under 4 inches.

Bob Terzuola's other considerations concerned the shape. Regarding the blade, it was obvious for him that it should be suitable as a daily tool and have good cutting qualities. The handle should fully cover the blade but also sit as comfortably and securely as possible in the hand. Furthermore, the handle should provide protection for fingers so that they don't slide onto the blade.

At the end of the design process* in the late 1980s, the ATCF model (Advance Technology Combat Folding knife) emerged. It stands out thanks to its very straight, simple design and an almost-4-inch-long blade with a light hollow grind, which gives it a versatile and elegant mixture of a drop point and spearpoint shape. It can be used equally well by right- and left-handers thanks to the blade lifter on both sides in the shape of a small disk. A liner lock made of titanium locks the blade.

The handle doesn't have marked finger grooves, meaning it can be easily turned in the hand. The clip has been mounted in tip-up style (so the tip of the blade points upward when the knife is clipped in place), and there is also a lanyard hole. A particularly elegant solution is the front handle end, which has been shaped to protect index fingers. It's shaped to fit perfectly with the thumb ramp on the back of the blade, so that when closed, the knife can be easily transported in a pocket.

Opposite: The knife makers who characterized the early years were Pat Crawford (Rekat Carnivore), Allen Elishewitz (CRKT Pharao), Bill Harsey (Gerber Airframe), Brian Tighe (CRKT My Tighe), RJ Martin (Kershaw Groove), and Ken Onion (Kershaw Tyrade).

---

* If you want to read about the development process of the **ATCF** in more detail, I recommend Bob Terzuola's very interesting book, *The Tactical Folding Knife*.

The ATCF has proven to be a timeless classic knife and has been continually in demand for over thirty years. To the regret of many knife enthusiasts, who don't have a budget large enough for an ATCF from Terzuola's workshop, there have only been a few limited series versions of the original design in all those years. Furthermore, Bob Terzuola has influenced countless other knife makers and industrial designers: the ATCF is rightly considered the forefather of the tactical folding knife. Other pioneers of the model (e.g., knife makers Bill Harsey, Pat Crawford, Harold "Kit" Carson, Allen Elishewitz, and John W. Smith) followed similar concepts.

TECHNICAL DEVELOPMENTS

The fundamental principle of a tactical folding knife has barely changed in the last thirty years. However, there have been revolutionary developments in construction and manufacturing. In 1999, CRKT brought the M16 on to the market, a design by the now-deceased knife maker "Kit" Carson. As a former professional soldier, he designed it as a lightweight folding knife for tactical use. The design was function based, while aesthetic aspects carried barely any importance. Nevertheless, or maybe for that exact reason, the knife was a success from the very beginning. The various M16 models have been sold in the hundreds and thousands and are still relevant today, twenty years later.

A reason for the success of the knife was the flipper—the tang ends in the shape of a small lever, which protrudes over the back of the handle of the closed knife. When you pull on this lever with your index finger, the blade is pushed some way out of the handle, and with a movement of the wrist the knife completely opens. The flipper is an opening system that is as simple as it's reliable, and using it is pure fun. Even though "Kit" Carson did not invent the flipper himself, which he openly admitted, this opening system only gained global popularity thanks to the M16.

A technological development of the 1990s that must not be forgotten is modern machine production; that is, blades are cut out by laser or water jet and then refined using computer-controlled (e-)grinders, while handles are completely milled by machine. Thanks to CNC machines, the relatively cheap production of more-complex shapes has become possible, which has created a previously unknown variety. Many manufacturers now started to produce series versions of the sought-after successful models designed by knife makers.

The next technological leap came at the start of the 2000s. Until then, industrially produced knife handles were generally very flat (i.e., they were simply made of flat materials). If there was any shape at all, it was just milled

FROM TACTICAL TO PRACTICAL: THE EVOLUTION | 2

The CRKT M16 designed by "Kit" Carson has been a global success for over twenty years. Thanks to the M16, the practical flipper mechanism has become very popular.

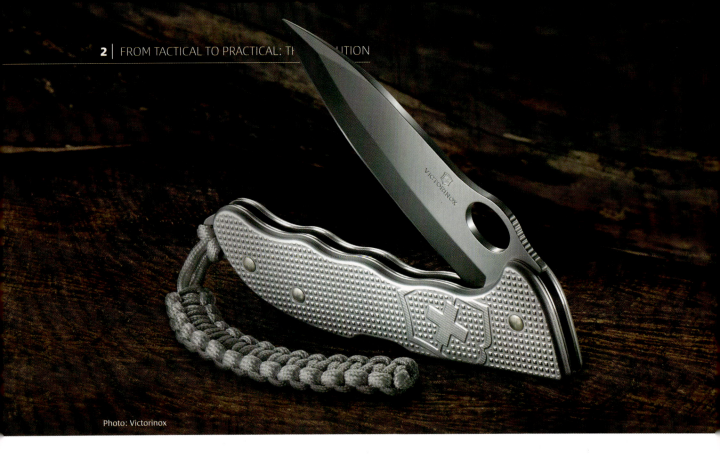

Photo: Victorinox

Even the tradition-steeped Swiss company Victorinox now has modern one-handed knives, such as the Hunter Pro M, in their range.

At Fox, modern knives are also manufactured using laser and CNC machines.

Photo: Fox

FROM TACTICAL TO PRACTICAL: THE EVOLUTION | 2

Photo: Pohl Force

grooves and hollows in the handles. In contrast, modern CNC milling machines can process a piece on several axes so that it's possible to create three-dimensional shapes.

The so-called 3-D milling revolutionized knife production, since it meant that the serial production of complexly structured handles was now possible. Previously, they could only be effortfully crafted by hand by knife makers. In the beginning, the 3-D-milled handles were reserved for high-quality and very expensive knives; for example, the first models by Zero Tolerance. Nowadays, 3-D-milling machines are so widespread that even affordable models are furnished with handles made from 3-D-milled G10.

A relatively new development is ball bearing washers for blades. Previously, most blades were on washers made of plastic or Teflon. On high-quality knives, the washers were disks made of phosphor bronze. As a result, there was a little frictional resistance when the knives were opened. In contrast, with ball bearings, there is practically no perceivable friction. The knife can be opened quickly and easily, and little maintenance is needed.

Knives with ball bearings brought about a real boom in flippers, which until then had been just one opening system among many. Today, the flipper is the most popular opening system. Thanks to the ball bearings, barely any additional movement of the wrist is necessary for the blade to easily fold out. Until the introduction of ball bearings, the knives using the flipper system were also additionally equipped

Thanks to ball bearings, modern folding knives can be opened much more easily and softly.

2 | FROM TACTICAL TO PRACTICAL: THE EVOLUTION

CUSTOMIZED

Often you can find a knife on the market that is almost perfect in every respect . . . apart from one or two small details. It's happened a lot even to me. Knife enthusiasts with practical skills often do DIY on the knife with a Dremel, a file, and sanding paper. Sometimes they even make completely new handle scales. Personally, I have no DIY skills; more like I have the proverbial two left hands. But fortunately, there are workshops that specialize in the tuning and customization of knives. One of them is the German company Cuscadi (Custom Scale Division), which is well known among knife enthusiasts.

Cuscadi has carried out modifications for me on the two knives in the image. The Contego (top) is a design by knife maker Warren Osborne. In its original form, the knife had handle scales made of black G-10, with a very rough "pocket eater" structure. I got Cuscadi to furnish it with handle scales made of coyote-colored G-10 with hand-sanded grooves.

The Benchmade Boost has great hand position; however, the series version only had a handle made of rubber-coated fiberglass, which I only found moderately attractive. For me, Cuscadi made suitable handle scales from multicolored python micarta. At the same time, the blade was given a stonewashed finish, and the springs of the assisted openers were also removed. Now it's a traditional one-hand knife with a completely new look (www.cucadi.de).

with a thumb pin or a similar blade lifter, but now they are frequently not added—many models only have the flipper mechanism.

Modern knife manufacturing and globalization also play a part in the final aspect of technical evolution: the price/performance ratio has become a lot better in recent years. This jump in quality has been observed in all price classes. You can buy a decent knife from approximately $20, really good models cost between $55 and $110, and in the premium class, for around $220 to $450 you can get a quality that previously could only be found in handcrafted knives. The reasons for this are, on the one hand, globalization—namely, production in China and Taiwan—and, on the other hand, the modern CNC-controlled milling and sanding machines.

Photo: CRKT

Knife maker Ken Onion examines the CRKT series model of his Outrage with a critical eye.

PRODUCTION IN THE FAR EAST

The most important production centers for modern pocketknives are found in the USA, in Maniago in Italy, and in Asia. In terms of volume, the sites in the Far East currently are the most important. Of course, knife production in the Far East is nothing new. It has been going on since the 1960s—first in Japan, then Taiwan, and today in China as well. However, back then, they liked to make a secret of it. Many prominent knife brands concealed the fact that their knives were produced in the Far East, but, at the same time, occasionally charged the same price as for knives manufactured in the USA or Europe. Very often, they relied on their well-known brand name being enough to hide the sometimes clearly lacking quality.

At the end of the 1990s, this practice started to become problematic for the companies: with the emergence of the internet, knife enthusiasts from around the world were able to swap experiences. In online forums, quality problems

3-D-milled handles made of titanium and G-10 show the whole variety and also the beauty of the modern folding knife. (Fox Wilson Extreme Light · Kizer Rattler · Rike Knight · Benchmade Rift · Benchmade Axis Flipper)

were discussed, and poor reviews spread at lightning speed through the click of a mouse. So it quickly made the rounds online if a famous brand charged a whopping $125 for a knife of basic quality, when you could buy the same quality from "no name" brands for $20 to $35. And people noticed if companies simply lasered their own brand name on the same model from China and the same knife was sold by different brands at very different prices.

The first producer that proactively addressed the topic of production in the Far East with a targeted marketing strategy was CRKT (Columbia River Knife & Tool), which was established in 1994. It commissioned the designs by famous knife makers such as Jim Hammond or Pat Crawford, to be produced in Taiwan (today in China), and brought them on to the market as series-produced knives at relatively affordable prices. The quality of these knives was comparatively high. The message was that US design plus Far East production made for a knife with a great price/performance ratio. The concept was a success, and within a few years, CRKT became one of the most important knife brands in the world.

Many producers learned from CRKT. Others created separate production lines: premium ranges were produced in the USA or Europe, while

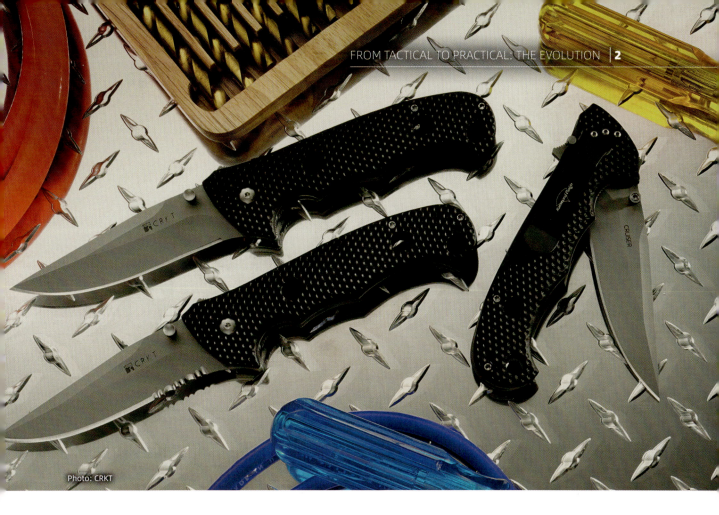

Photo: CRKT

more affordable ranges were manufactured in Taiwan or China.

After years of production for Western brands, the Chinese companies are now represented on international markets with their own brands. In China, there are also makers and designers who understand their work very well. The result is great knives with an excellent price/performance ratio. One of the first companies that had success on the international market in this way was Real Steel.

Nowadays, there are numerous Chinese brands that offer good products. One of the triggers for this boom was the amended weapons legislation in China that legalized modern one-hand knives. As a result, a large domestic market was created in China, and the demand massively increased.

A contrast to industrial production in China is the so-called mid-tech sector, where knife makers' workshops produce knives in small series runs. Their base is good-quality but machine-produced components. They are then further crafted by hand. Assembly, adaptation, and above all, the sharpening and fine sanding of the blade are done by an expert. Many of these hand-finished practical folding knives are essentially such mid-tech knives. The prices range between $450 and $775, depending on the material and features.

CRKT was the first company that openly advertised that US designs, such as the Cruiser by Jim Hammond, were produced in the Far East as more affordable versions.

TOOL OR WEAPON?

The development from the tactical to the practical folding knife brings us to this frequently asked question: When is a knife considered or not considered a weapon?

According to German law, "cutting weapons and thrust weapons" are objects that by nature are intended to injure persons. However, that only applies to very few knives. According to the German administrative provision to the Weapons Act (Verwaltungsvorschrift zum Waffengesetz–WaffVwV), it depends whether a knife "in its whole design is objectively intended to be used as a weapon to eliminate or reduce a human's ability to attack or defend." That is not the case when the blade "in its technical characteristics (length, width, shape) corresponds to that of a utility knife. As a rule, this can be assumed when the part of the blade protruding from the handle is shorter than 8.5 cm [3.3 inches] or is not double-edged."

Conversely, that does not mean that all larger knives are automatically weapons. Alongside the objective technical characteristics, the "prevailing public understanding" plays a role, which is influenced by the manufacturers' and designers' presentation and the marketing of the individual models, and also frequently by prejudices on the part of the justice authorities. In the case of doubt, you can apply to the German Federal Criminal Police Office for an assessment, of course for a fee.

The line between weapon and tool is blurred. As can be seen in the following example, even determinedly tactical features are not sufficient to automatically make a knife a weapon within the meaning of the law.

The weapon: A few years ago, the company Böker developed a pocketknife for self-defense in collaboration with close combat expert Jim Wagner.

The Reality-Based Blade was based on Wagner's self-defense system of the same name

TOOL

The Reality-Based Outdoor model was classified as a utility knife by the German Federal Criminal Police Office.

The back of the blade is only sanded, not sharp.

There is no blade lifter for one-handed opening.

Even though the handle is the same as a self-defense knife, the German authorities recognize that the nonslip shape is also useful for a utility knife.

According to the German authorities, the bellied shape of the blade is atypical for thrust weapons.

Despite the length of the blade being clearly over 8.5 cm, according to the German authorities it has the "overall impression of a utility knife."

FROM TACTICAL TO PRACTICAL: THE EVOLUTION

and was considered a weapon in several regards.

- The general shape was objectively recognizable as being designed for use as a weapon.
- The model was designated as a self-defense knife by the manufacturer.
- The knife was developed as a supplement to a specific close combat system and also bore this name.

The utility knife: For the Reality-Based Blade Outdoor, which in many respects is the same construction, there is an assessment from the German Federal Criminal Police Office (File No. SO11-5164.01-Z-238). It certifies that the knife is not a weapon despite sharing the characteristics of the original RBB. The German authorities came to the conclusion that the handle of the self-defense weapon is also advantageous for utility knives because it "offers a good hold when using it with wet hands."

An important difference is the blunt back of the blade: if sharpened, it serves "to increase the effect of stabbing." However with the RBB Outdoor it's only sanded, so that it only constitutes a "design element." The German authorities ascertained that "the manufacturer's intended purpose, the one-sided sharpened blade, the bellied blade shape (atypical for thrust weapons), and the fact that to open the blade, both hands are required speak against it being a weapon," meaning that "despite a blade length of approximately 10 cm, it gives the general impression of being a utility knife and therefore by nature" is not a weapon.

Although in this example, the two-handed opening is named as a criterion, one-handed knives are also not automatically regarded as weapons. In the German administrative provision to the Weapons Act (WaffVwV), it's expressly emphasized that they "can be useful utility knives."

WEAPON

The Reality-Based Blade was classified as a self-defense knife and is regarded by law as a weapon.

The gladius tip is named after the Roman sword and is designed for stabbing.

Blade lifter for one-handed opening

Ergonomic, non-slip handle with distinct hand protection

According to its description, the inwardly curved blade has been borrowed from the dagger.

The smooth recess leads the thumb to the blade lifter to enable fast opening.

The end of the handle is shaped so that the closed knife can be used as a strike weapon.

Photos: Böker

2 | FROM TACTICAL TO PRACTICAL: THE EVOLUTION

The range of high-quality knives is increasingly characterized by limited small series, using materials such as powder steel, titanium, and carbon fiber. The Balmis by Miguel Barbudo was produced by Reate in China on behalf of the German company Tools for Gents.

FROM TACTICAL TO PRACTICAL: THE EVOLUTION | 2

Photo: CRKT

CHAPTER 3
SCIENCE AND ART: THE DESIGN

Producing a pocketknife that meets all the requirements of a practical folding knife is not such a big challenge on paper. However, making a knife that can truly be described as an all-around success is a science of its own. The result is not just a question of production and material quality but is much, much more a matter of technical construction and a well-thought-out design. The best-quality material and the best production are of no use if the knife is poorly designed. Yet, a well-designed knife will also work, for example, if it's made of simple steel or there are still manufacturing marks on it.

The next step is to give a functional knife design an aesthetic shape. At the latest, this is where science becomes art. And in the knife sector, art is becoming increasingly more important, and that means increasingly more manufacturers are making the popular designs by famous knife makers as production editions.

"The whole is greater than the sum of its parts."
–Aristotle–

The magical "all-in-one-solution" doesn't exist in the world of knives either. You must be aware of that before purchasing—and most certainly before designing—a practical folding knife. Of course, compared to specialist knives for craftsmen or cooks, the pocketknife is intended as a universally deployable tool. However, they are still designed with particular purposes in mind.

In the murky depths of social media, you often come across users who use the slim flipper knives with ball bearings for bushcraft (e.g., to hack down branches or for batoning, using a baton-sized stick or mallet to repeatedly strike the spine of the knife). To do so, they use the knife like an ax for splitting wood. Afterward they are

Opposite: **The production Hootenanny from CRKT, designed by Ken Onion, excels thanks to its shape, which is as functional as it's aesthetic.**

3 | SCIENCE AND ART: THE DESIGN

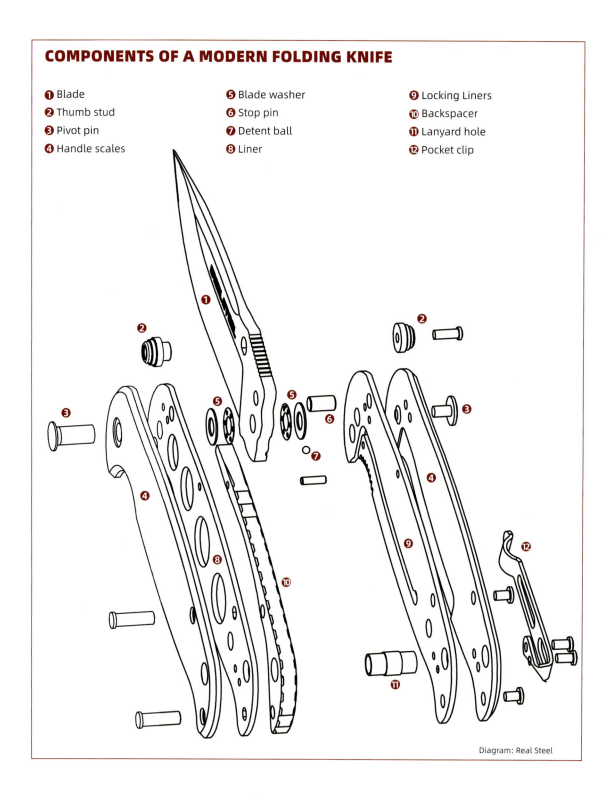

Diagram: Real Steel

shocked that, even on a high-quality knife, the blade no longer moves straight, it leans to one side, it no longer locks properly, or it shows other types of damage. In such cases, you can only say that an EDC flipper is not suitable for such work.

For this type of work, it's best to use an ax or a fixed blade knife, which do not have any mechanical weak points. Only in extreme emergencies should you use a particularly robust outdoor folding knife with tough locking (see chapter 6) for such heavy-duty work. An EDC pocketknife is intended for normal, everyday cutting work. Even practical folding knives should be used as intended. Incorrect usage sooner or later leads to damage.

Photo: MM/Oliver Lang

Even very robust folding knives, such as the Hunter Pro from Victorinox, are not really designed for primitive work such as batoning.

KEY QUESTIONS

The task of designing a practical folding knife can lead to the most-varied solutions, which are often incompatible with each other. Alongside the elementary technical requirements—one-handed operation, locking system, and clip, requirements regarding the function, appearance, and aesthetics play an important role. You can get very close to achieving these aspects by asking a few essential questions.

Wicked Cutter or "Sharpened Crowbar"?

There are two strongly opposing ideas regarding the purpose of a practical folding knife. The first believes that a pocketknife must withstand everything, even the worst abuse. Therefore, it should be as robust as possible, even if that is to the detriment of its cutting properties. The other concept emphasizes that a practical folding knife should primarily be an effective cutting tool. However, the lines are blurred—in the knife world, there are many models that hover between these two requirements. However, both designs, in their pure essence, lead to radically different knives.

3 | SCIENCE AND ART: THE DESIGN

THE "GAP"—AN AVOIDABLE NUISANCE

Looking at the individual elements of the whole knife system leads us to one point of criticism. Something that has barely any function but, for many knife enthusiasts, a huge annoyance is that there is a gap between the tang and the handle when the knife is closed. Although it's most frequently seen on back locks, it can also be found on liner, frame, and axis locks. Sometimes it's small and only visible on a second inspection, but sometimes it's really large and immediately noticeable.

In terms of functionality, the gap only has an effect when it's so large that the sharp edge of the tang gets snagged on pocket material and causes damage. In terms of aesthetics, it's simply always and constantly a nuisance. It sometimes feels like during the design process the knife industry only pays attention to a folding knife looking good when it's open. Many product managers at the manufacturers are not aware that the gap annoys a lot of customers.

In terms of construction, there is no reason for not closing this gap: to do so, you don't even need to change the design of the tang, the stop pin, or the locking mechanism—in most cases, it's enough to change the outer contours of the handle by 1 or 2 millimeters (0.05 inch).

Here is a good example showing two knives from the same producer: the Police (*top*) and the Stretch from Spyderco. The Police has enjoyed long-term success over decades for Spyderco, while the Stretch has also been in high demand for many years. The Stretch is somewhat smaller, but in terms of design, the two models are comparable: both have a flat polished blade with the thumb hole typical for Spyderco and a back lock. When closed, on the Police you can see a clear gap with the sharp-edged and protruding tang; in contrast, the Stretch has a harmonious transition in which the tang is concealed by the handle. The gap is therefore an annoyance that could quite easily be avoided by the knife producers.

"Sharpened crowbar" is a term in the knife community that describes the first idea very well. Followers of this approach assume that you should also be able to use a pocketknife for purposes that are actually covered by other tools (e.g., forcing open boxes or doors, hacking through small branches, and so forth). Therefore, folding knives based on this idea are generally very big and have a strong and solid construction. The 4mm (0.157-inch) blade width is often clearly exceeded. The blade is wide, and the grinding is not fine but robustly done. Even the handles and the pivot pins are made to be as large and solid as possible.

Objections to this idea are often based on the fact that a pocketknife will never achieve anything close to the stability of a fixed blade or that of a special tool, such as a machete, ax, or crowbar. It's not considered sensible to design a knife for tasks that it cannot properly fulfill.

According to the second idea, a "sharpened crowbar" can no longer reasonably fulfill the core purpose of a knife (i.e., cutting). The blade geometry is usually so robust in style that its cutting properties suffer—a knife is simply not an ax. And if the knife no longer cuts properly, it's no longer functional as a piece of equipment.

Therefore, there is a tendency toward pocketknives that have a blade geometry designed to cut well despite being large and robust. Of course, there

Knives of the same size but with very different cutting properties: "sharpened crowbar" (Schrade SCH301), robust blade geometry (Benchmade Vicar), and wicked cutter (Maxace Balance)

3 | SCIENCE AND ART: THE DESIGN

Above: Knives like the Buck Tops CSAR are primarily designed for heavy cutting work.

Opposite: From compact and light to large and heavy, there are different grades. (Gerber Slimsada · Real Steel Sea Eagle · Civivi Synergy3 · Pohl Force Four · Timberline Worden)

are also stages in between; for example, robustly constructed pocketknives for hunting and outdoor use, whose blade geometry is designed for the heavy-duty cutting needed during these activities.

Everyday Carry or Monster Folding Knife?

The bigger and more solidly a pocketknife is constructed, the more incorrect use it can withstand. However, it also means that these knives are too big and heavy to be comfortably carried in trouser pockets. Therefore, they are generally supplied with a belt holster. For example, soldiers who carry a knife on duty as part of their uniform or equipment often prefer such large models. However, carrying a folding knife in a holster on a belt is out of the question for most civilian users—the whole point of a pocketknife is that it can be carried in a pocket. Very few users want a large lump in their trouser pocket that could almost pull their trousers down because of its weight. A pocketknife that is too big or too heavy (or both) to carry in daily life is often simply left at home. And a pocketknife that you don't have on you when you need it is really pointless.

Accordingly, a practical folding knife should be large and robust but at the same time also as light and compact as possible, so that it can be comfortably carried each day in a trouser pocket—hence the term "EDC" (everyday carry). Furthermore, for many users it's important that it's not immediately visible that they are carrying a knife, since they don't want to shock the people around them. For that reason, many practical folding knives are kept flat so that they don't protrude too much out of trouser pockets but, where possible, disappear into the pocket (deep carry clip).

3 | SCIENCE AND ART: THE DES...

Not only compact gentleman's folding knives but also large knives can be very elegant. (Kansept Reverie · Bestech Starfighter · WE Knife 601 · Liong Mah Eraser)

"Tacticool" Or "Gray Man"?

In addition to size, shape, and color are decisive factors for how a knife is perceived. At the same time, the variety of shapes is practically endless. According to the motto "Knivestyle is lifestyle," the pocketknife is, if nothing else, a question of personal taste: Show me your knife and I will tell you who you are.

While many details on a knife are only noticeable at a second glance, other aspects are plain to see—very large blades, wild shapes, large recurves, and serrated edges suggest tactical features, even for the uninitiated. The color also plays a part: a black-coated blade and a camo handle give a military impression and hint that the knife is a weapon. Many people find the sight of such a knife disconcerting or even threatening. Therefore, a lot of knife enthusiasts have models that not only can be carried in pockets without notice but also have a discreet appearance. The art of such designs is to combine practical and tactical functions with an inconspicuous appearance. This principle is often described with the buzz phrase "Gray Man."

All considerations on selecting the correct knife are dependent on the person's individual circumstances: Do they work in construction, as a tradesperson, or in an open plan office? Factors such as clothing style and hand size also play a part, but also their personal social circle. However, the most important thing should be the user's own personal taste.

TYPICAL CONSTRUCTION MISTAKES

Poorly constructed knives have become noticeably rarer than they were a few years ago, but they are still very prevalent, above all in the lower price category from budget brands. Some problems, such as unfortunately shaped or sharp-edged handles, you feel the very first time you pick it up, and experienced knife users can recognize such problems just on the basis of the catalog photos.

In contrast, other problems are less obvious. For example, if the look of a popular or cool design is copied in the Far East without any understanding of the functional purpose behind the design features, then you get a knife that may look similar to the original but does not handle anywhere near the same.

Typical examples: A knife whose prototype's size and shape were designed to incorporate handle scales made of titanium but for reasons of cost has been produced in steel, which naturally makes it much too heavy. Or a design that is simply proportionally reduced without adapting the shape of the handle to the changed ratio to hand size, meaning the knife no longer sits well in the hand.

Whether a design should be discreet or wild and tacticool is a matter of personal taste. (Real Steel S571 Pro · WE Knife Beacon · WE Knife Chimera · CRKT Apoc)

3 | SCIENCE AND ART: THE DESIGN

FUNCTIONAL INTERPLAY

The biggest challenge in the design and construction of a pocketknife is to combine all the various requirements with each other. A practical folding knife should:

- cut as well and effectively as possible;
- be as robust, hard-wearing, and durable as possible;
- be as comfortable and as easy as possible to open and close with one hand;
- lock as safely as possible;
- be as slip-resistant and comfortable in the hand as possible;
- be as comfortable and as easy as possible to carry;
- be as easy as possible to bring out and put into the pocket;
- and, at the same time, look as good as possible.

To bring that all together sounds like the notorious "trying to square the circle"—and that is precisely what it is. To optimize one feature, you have to cut back on another feature. This means that a knife, even when using titanium, cannot be extremely robust and very large and at the same time also be superlight and comfortable to carry. Therefore, compromises must always be made in the design.

A functionally coherent design is an exact science. Creating a design that works on all levels so that it's not only super functional but also looks good goes above and beyond. With a folding knife, all details must be truly compatible with each other; a good pocketknife is a real art. Over the last twenty years, nearly all knife makers have started to produce popular designs by well-known knife makers in serial production.

In the next chapters, we will shine a light on the fundamental technical elements, each in their own chapter. Nevertheless, you should always bear in mind that a pocketknife is a whole system, in which the individual factors interact. According to the well-known belief of the philosopher Aristotle, a pocketknife as a whole is greater than the sum of its parts.

A typical example of this systematic thinking is the relationship between the blade and handle length. Both of these factors are directly dependent on each other.

In principle, longer blades are eminently desirable. However, because the handle has to safely enclose the folded blade and also house all the mechanics (pivot, blade washers, locking system, and spacer), it has to be 20% to 30% longer than the blade. If the handle ends up too big, you can no longer easily carry the knife in your pocket. But if the handle is too short, the knife doesn't sit well in your hand. In terms of function, the blade length is determined by the length of the handle. The art is to design a knife so that the ratio of blade length and handle length is as favorable as possible (i.e., achieving the maximum blade length within a defined handle length).

SCIENCE AND ART: THE DESIGN | **3**

Photos: Fox

Two examples of how the same knife can appear tactical or practical just by changing the color (Fox Suru · Trevor Burger Sierra Flipper)

Photo: Sharp by Coop

3 | SCIENCE AND ART: THE DESIGN

The Wild Weasel assisted opener was the first knife that CRKT produced in the USA.

A central element of knife construction is one-handed operation. For this purpose, there are several different mechanisms, such as blade lifters and flippers. How well they function does not only depend on their design but also on the interaction between the blade motion (i.e., the blade washers) and the locking system.

Since its introduction, the flipper has been a popular feature. However, it was only in combination with particularly smooth-moving blades on ball bearing washers that it developed into the system that currently dominates the market. And the frame lock only became prevalent when modern CNC milling machines enabled increasingly elaborate shapes for handles made of titanium or steel.

Not only should the handle be slip resistant and sit comfortably in the hand, but it should also be easy to carry in pockets. The clip should fix the knife in place in the pocket, but it also should not prevent it being pulled out or put back in. Furthermore, it must be shaped and attached so that it's felt as little possible in the hand and doesn't snag anywhere.

When cutting, people often place their thumb on the back of the blade, meaning that the blade and the back of the handle have to be shaped correspondingly and should ergonomi-

SCIENCE AND ART: THE DESIGN | 3

LOOK ON THE INSIDE

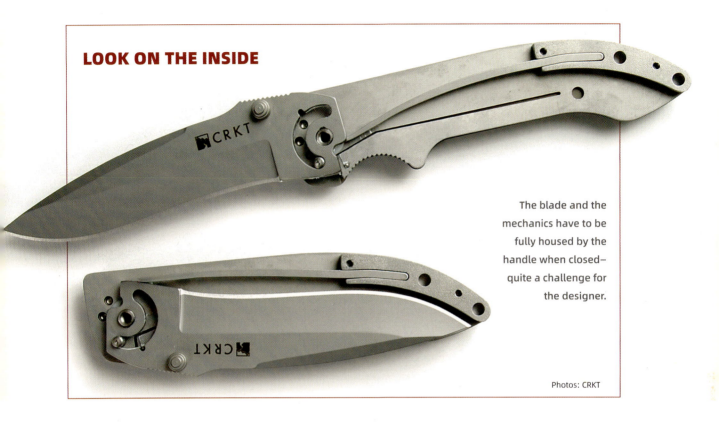

The blade and the mechanics have to be fully housed by the handle when closed—quite a challenge for the designer.

Photos: CRKT

cally flow into each other. And finally, a pocketknife should look harmonious and aesthetically pleasing both when it's folded and opened out.

With the exception of the back lock models, the majority of locking systems require an internal stop pin for the blade. The folded-out knife stops at this stop pin, and the locking system locks it in position. However, with flippers this pin is often positioned in the way of the blade tang when the knife is "snapped open." There are three solutions to this problem.

In some designs, the thumb pin on the blade also serves as a stop pin. This principle became popular thanks to knife maker Butch Vallotton. In some flipper knives that are designed according to this method, the thumb pins also no longer have any function as blade lifters but are only present as a stop pin for the blade.

The second solution is much more elegant but also more complex to produce: the stop pin is positioned close to the blade axis. This pin has its own channel milled into the tang. Or you can also do the exact opposite: the stop pin sits firmly anchored in the tang, while its guide groove is milled into the liner. That is known as a floating stop pin. Such designs are generally used on flippers that don't have a thumb pin.

3 | SCIENCE AND ART: THE DESIGN

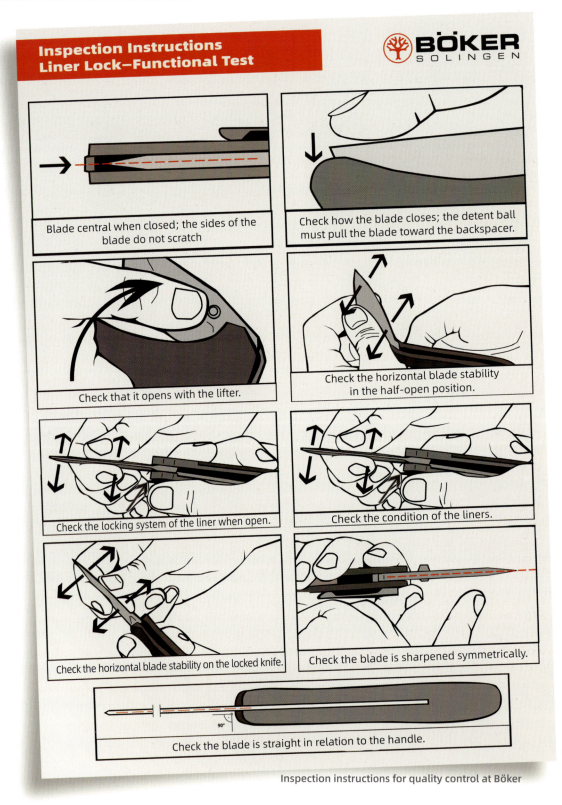

Inspection instructions for quality control at Böker

SCIENCE AND ART: THE DESIGN | 3

Photos: CRKT, Surefire

Different stop pin designs
❶ The thumb pin forms an external stop pin (CRKT Linchpin).
❷ The stop pin runs in a channel, which is milled into the tang.
❸ The stop pin has been affixed firmly in the tang and runs in a channel in the liners.

AFFORDABLE QUALITY

"You get what you pay for," as they say in America; in Germany, the saying goes, "If it costs nothing, then it's nothing." However, that does not necessarily mean that you have to pay a lot for a good pocketknife. By now, poor-quality knives have become more rare, even in the lower price ranges. If you do careful research before purchasing, you can still find a more-than-usable knife on a small budget. In the following, you will find a brief overview of the levels of quality currently offered on the market. Further explanation of the types of steel, handle material, and technical details are found in the next chapters. The stated price ranges reflect the situation at the time of printing.

Affordable Range (Approximately $10 to $35)

These knives are made of cheap material—for example, 420 steel, simple wood, FRN (fiberglass-reinforced nylon) and other plastics, and cheap aluminum alloys, as well as washers made of plastics or Teflon. In addition to imprecise sharpening and milling, problems also include poor finish, inaccurate fittings, and screws made of untreated steel. In this price range, you unfortunately find poorly designed knives, but also surprisingly good and very functional designs, too.

3 | SCIENCE AND ART: THE DESIGN

Entry-Level Range (Approximately $35 to $55)

In this class, you find better steel, such as 440C and sometimes even D2. The typical handle material is G-10, but aluminum and steel are also used. In addition to washers made of Teflon, there are often ball bearing washers. The fabrication is noticeably better but generally shows small imperfections. In this price range, there are often very decent day-to-day and work knives, but they are not designed for more-difficult work. Faulty construction is rare.

Lower Mid-Range (Approximately $55 to $135)

In this price class, considerably better-quality steels such as D2, N690, or 14C28N—and sometimes even cheap industrial Damascus steel—are used. The handle material is generally G10, but you can also often find steels, Micarta, or even carbon fiber. The workmanship is largely without mistakes, but you may still find small superficial flaws. In this price range, truly bad designs are extremely rare. In many cases, they are serial-produced models of designs by famous knife makers.

Upper Mid-Range (Approximately $135 to $220)

The blades in this price class are generally made of high-quality and stainless types of steel, such as N690, VG-10, or 154-CM, and sometimes even ground

Opposite: Series productions of knife makers' designs: Ivan Braginets (Real Steel Lynx), Flavio Ikoma (CRKT Fossil), Lucas Burnley (CRKT Butte), Eric Ochs (CRKT Avant-Tac), Jens Anso (MKM Goccia), Jesper Voxnaes (Böker Plus Field Folding knife)

THE KNIFE AS A WORK OF ART

In the case of handmade custom knives, even the uninitiated often very quickly recognize that they are works of art. You can tell from the special luxury materials and decorations, such as engravings. As soon as these embellishments are gone, then the special aesthetic of a knife design is not so easy to recognize.

Many knife makers and designers manage to give a knife a special look beyond the functional aspects. Although this special look comes into its own particularly well with certain materials, it can normally be recognized by the shape. Some designs have already enjoyed cult status for decades and are popular and sought after throughout the whole community. Other designs delight a smaller but very loyal fan base.

The designs of the famous and in-demand knife makers have already been serial-produced by the industry for decades. The range includes very simple serial models in standard-quality and high-quality models right up to very expensive premium knives.

Whether as limited special editions or a normal part of the range, each year the manufacturers bring new designer knives on to the market.

1 | SCIENCE AND ART: THE DESIGN

Photo: Pohl Force/Sebastian Lucke

Damascus steel. They open by using bronze disks or ball bearing washers. The handles are made of high-quality wood, G-10, Micarta, and occasionally titanium. The workmanship is normally flawless. As a rule, the designs by knife makers are used.

High-End Range (Approximately $220 to $330)

In this price class, you generally only find blades made of powder steel, such as S35VN or Damascus steels. Titanium, carbon, and Micarta are the materials of choice for the handles. Titanium handles are often also processed and milled on the inside, while the blades generally slide on ceramic ball bearing washers. There should be no superficial flaws at all in the workmanship.

Luxury Range (From $330)

The blades are made of the highest-quality powder steel, such as M390, Damascus steel, or powder metallurgical Damasteel. The handles are made of luxury carbon fiber materials or titanium, and for individual elements, titanium Damascus is used. These knives are flawless right down to the finest tolerances and enjoy high-quality workmanship.

Opposite: **Even with a high percentage of machine production, as with Lion Steel in Maniago, the final assembly of modern folding knives is still done by hand.**

Many companies launch very luxurious models as limited editions. This MKM Arvensis in Damascus steel and titanium costs over $650.

Photo: MKM

3 | SCIENCE AND ART: THE DESIGN

SCIENCE AND ART: THE DESIGN | **3**

Even knives costing less than $50 are often surprisingly functional and perform really well as everyday tools. (Black Ice Njola II · Marser Städter-1 · Cold Steel Pro Lite · Ruike Hussar · Ontario RAT-1 · Elite Force EF 133)

Photo: CRKT

CHAPTER 4

THE HANDLE: THE CONNECTION BETWEEN MAN AND KNIFE

When I was young, if I had been asked whether the blade or the handle was the most important thing on a knife, I would have answered without hesitation that it would be the blade. But after gaining more experience, I would now answer that in my opinion the handle is more important.

Of course, a knife also needs a functional blade. But a knife is a hand tool. And by definition, in order to use it, you have to be able to hold it in your hand. Using a knife with a blunt blade is a real annoyance but it can be very easily corrected by resharpening it.

Yet, a knife with a poor handle that painfully presses into your hand when you are working, turns in your hand, or even slips out of your hand is a considerably larger problem. A handle that sits comfortably in your hand is essential; after all, the handle is the connection between man and knife!

"Intelligence is a dual-edged sword made of hard steel and a sharpened blade, but character is the handle, and without the handle it's without value."

– Friedrich von Bodenstedt –

THE HANDLE DESIGN

It all starts with the design, and with it, the fundamental question of function. The handle of a pocketknife must perform important tasks:

- it must be safe, above all slip resistant, and sit as comfortably as possible in your hand when working,
- it must prevent fingers from slipping onto the blade while you're working,
- it must be easy to carry in trouser pockets and be pulled out and put back in as easily as possible,

Opposite: **Knife makers such as Ken Onion know that to sit comfortably and safely in your hand, the handle must be sufficiently large. (CRKT Homefront)**

Photo: Böker

Thanks to modern CNC milling machines, handles can now be made in almost any shape.

- it must house the mechanics of the knife, and
- it must safely cover the closed blade.

While the last two points depend on the type of locking mechanism and the shape of the blade, the first three points are independent design factors, which often contradict each other. Although a handle that is as small, slim, flat, and smooth as possible can be easily carried and put in and pulled out of trouser pockets, it sits less comfortably in the hand when you're working. There are also handles that have been especially ergonomically shaped to accommodate the fingers and the curves of the palm.

The market offers both extremes, but ideally the shape represents a compromise between the different requirements of ergonomics and carriability.

The handle of a pocketknife encompasses four factors of functional design that interplay with each other:

- side profile
- thickness
- curve
- surface texture

There are several methods of giving a handle an ergonomic profile. Sometimes, it's enough to incorporate a single index finger groove to give the

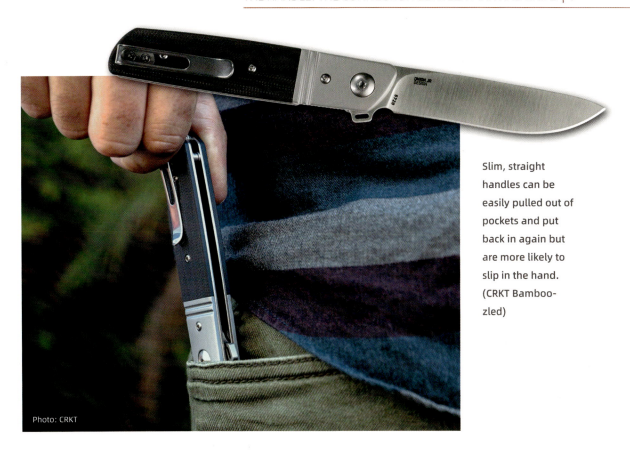

Slim, straight handles can be easily pulled out of pockets and put back in again but are more likely to slip in the hand. (CRKT Bamboozled)

Photo: CRKT

hand extra control for light cutting work. If you need to do tougher work, the whole handle must be ergonomically shaped. In order to fit the curves of the palm, such handles are often more curved and have a thicker butt. Sometimes, it may also be shaped as a small hook to prevent the hand from slipping backward.

Even the thickness of the handle will have also been thought through. A rather slim and flat handle does not appear bulky in trouser pockets but does not sit well in the hand. The slimmer and flatter the knife, the more force required when working to prevent the handle from slipping out of the hand.

Knives that are produced by hand have always had shaped handles, which fit well into the curve of the hand. In the case of industrial mass-produced models, such handles were rare for a long time. Above all, when handle materials such as steel, aluminum, or G-10 were milled out of plates and polished, it usually led to very flat handle scales. Only with cast handle scales made of aluminum or plastic could other shapes be produced at an economically reasonable cost. That changed as 3-D milling machines spread and became more popular. Today, you can even frequently find titanium handles with curved surface.

IDEAL FOR MY HAND

Just like shoes, where not every style suits every foot shape despite being the correct size, sometimes a knife handle will not suit every hand. Determining factors are not just the size of the hand, but also its individual shape, as well as many different ways of gripping the handle. Ideally, the handle shape would be tuned exactly to my hand and my personal preferences. Just as with this knife.

This folding knife was made by knife maker Stefan Steigerwald, using my own design (www.steigerwald-messer.de). It was important that the carbon handle would be very shallow and would bulge out of the trouser pocket as little as possible. The side profile is tailored perfectly to my hand. At the same time, it had to be considered that the swedge is sharpened. This part of the RWL-34 blade had to be completely covered when the knife is folded, so that the sharp edge would not protrude from my trouser pocket.

Stefan perfectly executed my specifications. That was a few years ago now, and in the meantime, knife technology has developed further, and I hold knives in a very different way. Once again, I have some new ideas for the "perfect pocketknife." As soon as I have some more time to sketch it, another idea will actually become reality.

THE HANDLE: THE CONNECTION BETWEEN MAN AND KNIFE | 4

Even flat knife handles can achieve better antislip properties thanks to texturing. Milled grooves on the back and underside of the handle are typical. Handle materials such as G-10 and Micarta can be given a rough structure by sandblasting or rough sanding. With the advent of modern 3-D milling machines, increasingly complex surface structures in these materials, even on very affordable knives, can be found.

Another very important element sits on the transition from the handle to the blade: the thumb rest. It's generally positioned on the back of the blade and consists of a section with more or less heavy jimpings. For many models, this rest is shaped as a slight upward ramp so that the thumb is not placed on the actual spine of the blade. Sometimes the blade spine has several rests, so that when doing heavy cutting work, you can place the thumb farther forward.

The handle underside is sometimes shaped so that you can hold the knife using the so-called forward grip technique, where the index finger is placed in a choil on the ricasso of the blade. It allows for more control when doing fine cutting work.

Index finger recesses, curved handle backs, and ergonomically contoured profiles ensure a safe hold. (CRKT Remedy · Böker Plus Masada · Zero Tolerance 0630 · Benchmade Mini Skirmish)

4 | THE HANDLE: THE CONNECTION BETWEEN MAN AND KNIFE

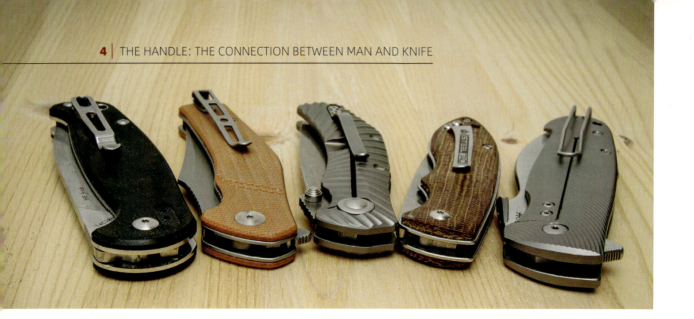

Modern CNC machines don't just shape handles from flat materials but can also give them curved profiles.

THE HANDLE CONSTRUCTION

For modern folding knives, there are three basic types of handle construction.

Liner and handle scales: For most knives on the market, the handle scales are screwed to an approximately 1.5mm (0.06-inch) thick steel or titanium liner.
Self-supporting handle: The handle scales are made of material several millimeters thick, without additional liners. You usually find these solutions in handle scales made of aluminum, steel, or titanium. With frame lock models, two different types of materials are often combined: the back scale with a frame lock is made of steel or titanium, while the front side is made of materials, such as G-10 or carbon fiber.
Handle made from a single piece of material: In rare cases, the handle is shaped from a single solid block of

The thumb rests, which are generally grooved, can be designed and shaped very differently.

THE HANDLE: THE CONNECTION BETWEEN MAN AND KNIFE | 4

Knife handles made of titanium plus a mixture of steel and G-10, which were decorated with 3-D-milled structures. (Viper Italo · Defcon TD 1001 · Zero Tolerance 0920 · CRKT Fossil · Kizer Dukes)

4 | THE HANDLE: THE CONNECTION BETWEEN MAN AND KNIFE

In this example, the blade base and handle are shaped so that you can place your index finger in the choil in front of the handle. (Stedemon ZKC-D01)

For many designs, the backscale and the frame lock are made of steel or titanium, but the front handle scale is made of a different material. (CRKT Tuna)

titanium, carbon fiber, or G-10. In terms of functionality, it has limited benefits regarding stability but means a lot less screws. A knife handle from one piece of material is above all an expression of a particularly high-quality and intricate production.

In contrast to old-school pocketknives, modern practical folding knives are generally not riveted but screwed instead. That has several benefits: you can take the knife apart for cleaning, maintenance, and adjusting, as well as for possible repairs or tuning. However, some manufacturers don't want owners to tinker with their knives. In such cases, it voids the guarantee.

The so-called bolsters are a detail of traditional pocketknives that can also be found on many modern practical folding knives. Originally, the bolsters were a thickening on metal handle frames. Bolsters were cast from brass or nickel silver or separately riveted to the liners. They serve to strengthen the head and end parts of the handle—particularly in the area where the blade pivots.

On modern knives, bolsters are used, above all, for aesthetic reasons. They are made of steel, aluminum, titanium, or even carbon fiber and screwed in place. For some models, the bolsters are, together with the liner, milled out of a single piece of steel or titanium.

Two versions of the Spyderco Starmate: the first with a self-supporting handle made of G-10, and the second with liners made of steel.

4 | THE HANDLE: THE CONNECTION BETWEEN MAN AND KNIFE

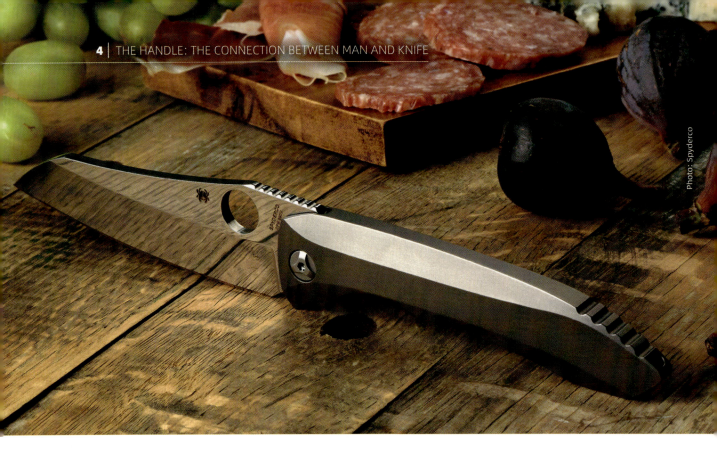

Photo: Spyderco

The handle of the Spyderco Paysan is milled from a single solid block of titanium.

Different designs of the lanyard hole

With the exception of back-lock models and handles made from a single piece, the backspacer is usually found on the back of a practical folding knife's handle between the handle scales or liners. It's often specially shaped or grooved in order to improve its ergonomic and antislip properties. As a rule, the backspacer leaves a fair-sized part of the handle back open, so that it's possible to clean the inside of the knife without having to take it apart. Instead of a solid backspacer, there may also be just two or three small roll-shaped spacers (standoffs) in the knife. In this case, the back of the handle remains completely open, which is particularly good for maintenance. In addition, it also means a reduction in the weight of the knife.

In most models, there is a lanyard hole at the back end of the handle to attach a strap. The hole can be used as a hand strap to protect against loss. Often, the strap has been tied in elaborate knots and is used as an aid to pull the knife or simply as personal decoration. A lot of users dislike the appearance of the hole, so other solutions are often found. In some knives it's integrated decoratively in the backspacer, or the hole is positioned on the inside and can't be seen from the outside.

TORX AND LOCTITE

With only a few exceptions, all modern folding knives are assembled using Torx screws. As a rule, they are size T8 for the pivot pin and size T6 for the remaining screws. If you only want to maintain your knife when needed, then the tools from knife maintenance kits or a simple precision screwdriver kit are normally adequate. They can usually be purchased cheaply and offer several bits in small screwdriver sizes. However, if you want to readjust your knife, you should invest a few dollars in a high-quality Torx screwdriver. Many affordable knives only have basic-quality screws. Good screwdrivers help prevent the screwhead from being stripped.

Large amounts of liquid screw fixer (Loctite) are often used by manufacturers of more affordable knives. Upon taking a knife apart, if you feel resistance when unscrewing a screw, you should never under any circumstance apply brute force, since there is a high risk of destroying the screws. Instead, you can turn the screw fixer back to liquid by applying heat. To do so, heat the screw for about three minutes with a hairdryer on its highest setting.

Different solutions for the backspacer and standoffs.

Photo: CRKT

4 | THE HANDLE: THE CONNECTION BETWEEN MAN AND KNIFE

Bolster with bolster lock (WE Knife Curvaceous · Ruger Hollow Point), traditional steel bolster (Spyderco Schempp Persian), designer bolster made of carbon (Defcon Mako)

The handle of the WE Knife 910 is screwed together on the back in a very unique way.

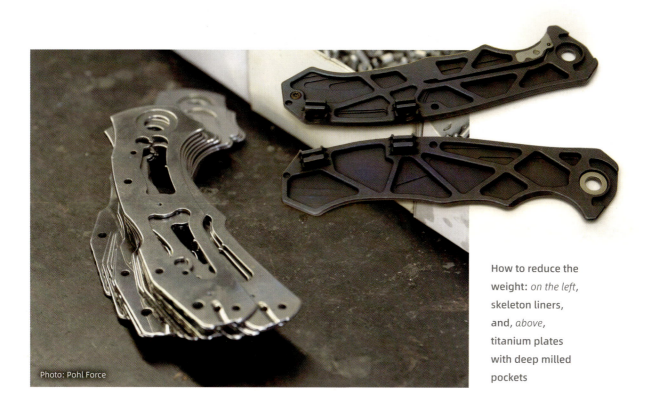

How to reduce the weight: *on the left*, skeleton liners, and, *above*, titanium plates with deep milled pockets

To reduce the weight of the knife, steel liners are often perforated or skeletonized. For handles made of steel and titanium, there is a further option to reduce the weight by integrating recessed pockets on the inside of the handle scales. That's a sign the knife has been elaborately crafted. Since by nature it's an intensive work process both in terms of time and machines, many manufacturers unfortunately do not go to this effort—since it cannot be seen on the outside.

THE HANDLE MATERIALS

Fiberglass Composite / FRN

In online shops, you often see the abbreviation FRN. It stands for fiberglass-reinforced nylon. As a rule, the starting material is polyamide, which is very solid and resistant to chemicals. Through admixing very thin glass fibers of approximately 0.1–0.5 millimeters (0.004–0.02 inches) in length, both the tensile strength and the resilience of the polyamide are considerably increased. Glass fibers are resistant to aging, weatherproof, chemical resistant, incombustible, and above all, very resilient.

Some of these fiberglass composites are known by their own brand names, like, for example, Zytel from Dupont. Benchmade and Cold Steel often use Grivory, which uses polyphthalamide as its basis.

4 | THE HANDLE: THE CONNECTION BETWEEN MAN AND KNIFE

Handle scales made of molded FRN (SOG Vision Arc · CRKT Ruger Follow Through · Fox Predator II · Cold Steel Counter Point 1)

From the knife maker's point of view, this composite's great benefit is that it can be molded into shape. That is why it's frequently used for affordable knives, which are produced in large numbers. However, there are initial high investment costs for the injection molds. Changes are also not easy to enact, because every time a change is made, a new injection mold is required. FRN is cheap, robust, and durable.

Molding also means that the curved handle shapes can be affordably produced. From the knife user's point of view, a disadvantage is that FRN can end up being smooth and slippery, depending on the mold and texture it creates. Furthermore, the material also clearly feels like plastic.

G-10

In principle, G-10 (or G10) is also a fiberglass composite, but in the world of knives, it occupies its own category because, unlike FRN, it's not molded but is milled from solid material and then sanded into shape. G-10 is a laminate made of woven fiberglass sheets and epoxy resin.

Like FRN, G-10 is resistant to weather and chemicals. However, thanks to the woven structure, it's considerably denser and more tough. G-10 is age resistant and extremely robust and needs almost no care. Furthermore, thanks to its woven construction, the material provides a better feeling of grip. The benefit for the industry is that G-10 can be

processed with CNC milling machines, and therefore, small runs of knives can also be economically produced.

G-10 in a material thickness of 3 to 4 mm (0.11 to 0.16 in.) is normally mounted on to the liners as handle scales. A design using self-supporting G-10 with a high material thickness is relatively rare. The characteristic, antislip surface is created by blasting. A blast of sand, glass beads, or corundum removes the soft epoxy resin from the surface so that the structure becomes rough. Depending on the weave type of the fiberglass sheets and the blasting method, slightly different nonslip surface textures are produced. When you sand and polish G-10, the surface appears like polished Micarta.

G-10 is produced in different colors, but for a long time classic black was dominant. The additional ability to produce G-10 in combined color tones gives rise to interesting possibilities. The different layers have different colors. Curved and decorated with unusual patterns, G-10 has a very different optical appearance to other blasted flat material. 3-D milling really brings out the layers of different colored G-10. In this way, handles are produced that offer a combination of functional material properties, an antislip structure, and a great appearance. A few years ago, 3-D-milled G-10 was a hallmark of high-end brands such as Zero Tolerance. Since many Chinese producers acquired milling

Different G-10: Black green (Ruike P841-L); convex-shaped, and smooth-polished (Spyderco Tropen); coyote brown and blasted (Fantoni HB1); blasted with milled grooves (Steel Will Barghest); and 3-D-milled (Civivi Dogma)

Different Micarta: Canvas Micarta (MKM Goccia · Steeltax No. 2 · Fox Geco), Burlap Micarta (QSP Hawk), Canvas Micarta with carbon bolsters (QSP Gannet)

machines, 3-D-milled G-10 can now also be really frequently found in mid-range and affordable knives.

Micarta

Actually a registered brand name, Micarta is used for all composite materials that consist of laminates of synthetic resin with cloth or paper. It has been used for knife handles since the 1960s and can be easily processed with milling or sanding machines. Micarta offers many benefits: it's dimensionally stable as well as resistant to weather, dampness, temperature changes, and many chemicals.

Since natural materials form the basis of Micarta, it produces a warm, natural grip feeling of the type you would otherwise only feel with wood. Compared to G-10 and carbon, the tensile strength and weather resistance of Micarta is evidently lower, but due to its surface feel, its grip, and its natural appearance, the material has its fans.

There are innumerable types of Micarta. The basis is formed of absorbent natural materials, which can be dyed in various colors. These materials are impregnated with phenol resin and then formed into bundles of many layers. The bundles are pressed and then the resin is left to harden.

Depending on the starting material, there are four main different types of Micarta:

IVORY SUBSTITUTES

In times gone by, ivory used to be a popular handle material for high-quality knives. The greed for the "white gold" ultimately brought elephants to the edge of extinction and the ivory trade was prohibited. Since then, fossil mammoth ivory has frequently been used for handmade custom knives, and substitute materials with a similar appearance have been used on practical folding knives.

Elforyn is a mixture of various materials and synthetic resin. The material can be milled and sanded and is resistant to dampness and various chemicals. Elforyn Super Tusk is constructed so that it even imitates the specific growth rings of real ivory: the so-called Schreger lines, which appear in the cross sections. Elforyn is colorfast, while real ivory yellows over the years and as result takes on its characteristic shade. Those who like this antique appearance are best off choosing Antique Ivory Micarta. This originally creamy-white paper Micarta also yellows over the course of time. Some types take on a golden-yellow shade.

The intensity of the yellowing depends on, among other things, the type of paper used. In this regard, you need to be careful: normal white paper Micarta is not the same as Antique Ivory Micarta because it does not yellow.

Handmade folding knife with titanium bolster and handle scales made of ivory Micarta (cooperation between André Thorburn and André van Heerden)

Photo: Sharp by Coop

- **Linen Micarta** is made of fine to medium cloth. It has a subtle but definitely antislip woven structure and is comparatively thick.
- **Canvas Micarta** is made from rough canvas. It has a very distinct woven structure and is used above all for outdoor and tactical knives.
- **Burlap Micarta** is very clearly and rather roughly structured. It's rather slip proof and also has a very characteristic appearance that is much loved by many knife enthusiasts.
- **Paper Micarta** possesses both the finest and thickest surface in terms of optics and haptics. It's primarily used for luxury knives. Richlite is a variety that comprises different colored pieces of paper glued together, which results in a very vibrant and attractive pattern.

THE RUINED WOOD HANDLE

Compared to modern handle materials, natural wood is a fairly delicate material for knife handles. Once at a barbeque, I lent my pocketknife to the "grillmeister" to cut the sausage packaging—it was the "original" Viper by Tecnocut with wooden handle scales. Unfortunately, instead of folding the blade closed and popping it in his pocket, or just giving it back to me, without thinking he put it in a puddle of beer...

Within a short space of time, the handle scales were soaked, swollen, and in the end, completely warped. Even very careful drying out could not save it. That was a big lesson for me.

Depending on the surface treatment, canvas and jute Micarta as well as the rougher linen Micarta are really porous. Although they are resistant to moisture, they do absorb some. As a result, when doing sweat-inducing work, the handle has a particularly safe and comfortable feeling. Over time it develops a certain patina, there are slight discolorations, and the surface becomes somewhat smoother. In order to return it to its original state, use a rough cleaning sponge and some washing-up liquid.

Wood

Basic wood types are used above all on affordable pocketknives, while for high-quality knives, more luxurious types of wood are used. Wood is beautiful to look at and very nice to touch. But there are serious disadvantages: the natural material "moves" and may warp over time, since it's not moisture- or weatherproof. Therefore, when you're doing hard work, the knife is unavoidably exposed to sweaty hands. Even if you take care of a wooden handle and regularly oil it, it's not resistant to moisture.

A functional alternative to natural wood is stabilized wood. To create it, a vacuum procedure is used to suck the air out of the wood's pores, then fluid synthetic resin is pressed deep into the pores, with great pressure. Stabilized wood shows the same grain as natural wood, but similar to plastic, it's not easily damaged by moisture and weather. It's primarily used on luxury, handmade knives. However, if you still want natural wood, very hard and dense woods that

Opposite: **Back-lock folding knife with 3-D-milled handle scales made of bocote wood (Pohl Force Mike Five)**

The optical and haptic effect of the Micarta surface depends not only on the base material but also on how it's processed. It can be sanded at different grain grades to achieve the desired grip. Micarta is often polished smooth to achieve a surface as fine and as compact as possible on luxury knives. On robust outdoor knives, the surface is often blasted with glass beads so that it's as slip resistant as possible.

Carbon with traditional woven structure (Zero Tolerance 0804CF); wild carbon (Real Steel Sidus); marbled carbon (Fox 40° Anniversary); copper shred carbon (SteelTac No. 1); curved, polished woven structure (Real Steel Lynx)

only move a little are best; for example, desert ironwood, grenadilla, or ebony.

Carbon Fiber

When talking about knives, carbon is a simple way to say carbon fiber laminate. Carbon fibers are significantly thinner than glass fibers, but much firmer and more resilient. Above all, its tensile strength is extremely high. Of all the handle materials, carbon has the best resilience/weight ratio. It's extremely light and at the same time extremely firm. Carbon is about four times as resilient as aluminum and has a similar tensile strength to steel, but it's about 80% lighter. In addition, carbon is fully corrosion resistant.

Compared to fiberglass, carbon fiber is significantly more expensive both in regard to the material price and the cost of processing; machines and abrasive materials suffer heavy wear and tear from carbon fiber. Furthermore, the sanding dust from carbon fiber is hazardous to health. Therefore, handles made of carbon fiber are generally only found on knives in higher price classes. For reasons of cost, sometimes a laminate of G-10 and carbon fiber is used (e.g., the inner sides of the handle scales are made of G-10, and the outer, visible sides are made of carbon fiber).

To produce carbon fiber laminates, carbon fibers with a diameter of just a few micrometers are combined with so-called filament yarn, which is then used to weave the sheets. Several layers of these sheets are then laminated with epoxy. It creates a typical weave pattern, which can be easily seen after sanding.

Carbon fibers can also be mixed with resin in other ways so that optically more-beautiful effects are created. For example, marbled carbon with a marble effect is particularly popular. By adding additional material, specific effects can be achieved; for example, for the lightning strike effect, thin threads of brass are woven in, and for the copper shred effect, the same is done with copper scrapings. In another way, using colored resin as the binding agent, different effects are created instead of just the simple black carbon types; for example, the marbled black and red, and the red lava effect.

Steel

Handle scales made of steel are used mainly in affordable frame lock knives. Since edge-holding ability is not important for handles, it's possible to use affordable and stainless steels; for example, the AISI steel types 410 and 420 are popular. Steel is extremely tough and resistant to chemicals and weathering. Furthermore, it also lends itself well to being processed with machines. Steel and titanium not only are anodized but are also often given a different finish for the sake of appearances—more in the chapter on blade steels.

However, steel also has its disadvantages as a material for handles. Compared to other materials, it's very

For this handle, knife maker Kirby Lamber tused lightning strike with brass wire and marbled carbon.

Photo: Sharp by Coop

4 | THE HANDLE: THE CONNECTION BETWEEN MAN AND KNIFE

In the more affordable ranges, handles made of steel are widespread. (CRKT Up and At Em)

heavy. In addition, a steel handle feels very cold, which can be very uncomfortable, especially in low temperatures. One of the biggest problems is that steel is rather smooth and slippery. To counteract that, the knife handle should have either a pronounced ergonomic profile or an antislip texture.

Aluminum

In the 1990s, handle scales made of aluminum were very widespread on pocketknives, but they have become rarer. One of the biggest advantages is that aluminum only weighs a third of steel. Although aluminum is less tough than steel, it's anti-magnetic and rust resistant. When exposed to air, untreated aluminum alloys form a silver-gray oxide layer a few nanometers thick, which adds extra protection against corrosion. Aluminum's disadvantages are that it's significantly more sensitive than steel or titanium and wears considerably faster.

In most online shops and catalogs, the material is often only described simply as "aluminum"; however, there are different alloys in different quality classes. For knives that are produced in large numbers, the handle scales are often die-cast, using aluminum alloys with a copper content. This method is cheap but has the disadvantage that during the die-cast process, small air bubbles may appear, and these bubbles are natural weak points. Particularly cheap alloys are also known internationally as light metals.

High-quality knives generally use aluminum alloys with magnesium and silicon, which have a high tensile strength and are both tough and resistant to corrosion. They can be die-cast into shape, but because they can also be machine-processed very well, the knife handles are generally milled from a solid block. The most famous of these AlMgSi alloys is called anticorodal. A different alloy is the so-called hardened aluminum (6061 T6), also colloquially known as aircraft aluminum. In addition to silicon, it also contains approximately 0.7% iron as well as up to 1.2% manganese and is heat-treated. Unfortunately for the

Different folding knives with aluminum handles (Leatherman Free K4 · CRKT Sampa · Buck Marksman · Böker Plus Warbird)

knife purchaser, it's normally not evident which alloy has been used for a specific model. Although this knowledge often only has little relevance to practice, be aware that aluminum sometimes has significant differences in quality.

As a rule, the surfaces of these milled aluminum alloys are anodized. Thanks to the anodic oxidization, they develop a colored protective layer. This procedure is often also known as electrolytic oxidization.

Contrary to galvanic coating, with anodization the uppermost micrometers of the metal transform into a corrosion- and abrasion-resistant oxide. The surfaces become particularly hard wearing and corrosion resistant through so-called hard anodizing, which creates an oxide layer that is approximately twice as thick than with normal anodizing.

Titanium

Handles on expensive knives are often made of titanium. Thanks to modern, CNC-controlled, 3-D milling machines, titanium knife handles can be made in any shape and to every taste. They can also be anodized to appear as different colors. This material combines the positive properties of steel and aluminum, and that is why titanium is the material of choice for high-quality frame-lock folding knives.

Compared to aluminum, titanium is over 50% heavier but also twice as strong and resilient. Compared to steel, titanium is a good 40% lighter, and similarly sturdy. Titanium is anti-magnetic, anti-allergic, and absolutely stainless.

Similar to aluminum, a protective oxide layer forms on the titanium surface upon contact with oxygen. Due to considerably lower heat conduction, titanium does not feel metallically cold, but "warmer" than aluminum or even steel. The disadvantages of titanium are the price of the material and higher processing costs. Just like carbon, titanium leads to more wear and tear on the production tools.

For a knife handle, you could use very soft pure titanium ("grade 2" according to the US system). However, a reliably functioning frame-lock requires a harder alloy. Therefore, the very hard, corrosion-resistant alloy Ti-6Al$_4$V ("Grade 5" according to the US system) with approximately 6% aluminum and approximately 4% vanadium is often used.

A special type of titanium is the very expensive Damascus titanium. Two different types of color-anodized titanium are welded together, using a special procedure. The resulting colorful pattern resembles the famous Damascus steel (see chapter 10). The functional properties are the same as normal titanium. Often the Timascus variety is used. Its name and production procedure have been patented.

GLASS BREAKERS

Glass breakers are intended to break security glass on vehicles in the case of an accident. This feature mounted on the end of the handle was originally only found on rescue knives for the fire brigade or technical emergency services, or on tactical knives for the military. Nowadays, they are also seen on civilian folding knives, since at the end of the day, an accident could occur at any time.

On affordable knives, the glass breaker is generally made of hardened steel, and as a result, they are often unfortunately ineffective because they generally get squashed flat against the safety glass. Glass breakers that work consist of a sharp cone made of tungsten carbide (*photo*). Alternatively, an extremely hard nanoceramic is used.

For the blade of the Shamwari, knife makers Gareth and Jason Bull used Damascus steel, and for the handle scales, they used Timascus.

Titanium handles on expensive knives: 3-D milled (QSP Woodpecker · Böker Plus Stingray), 3-D milled and color anodized (Zero Tolerance 0606CF), and with carbon inlays (Reate K3)

THE HANDLE: THE CONNECTION BETWEEN MAN AND KNIFE | 4

Photo: CRKT

CHAPTER 5

EDGY SHAPES: THE BLADES

A knife's main purpose is to cut, and its blade must be optimized for exactly that. But what does that mean? Which blade cuts well and why? And what are the limits to this optimization? In this chapter, we'll try to present the science of blade shapes and edge geometry in an understandable way.

"The tongue is the only tool that gets sharper with use."

–Washington Irving–

THE BLADE SHAPES

The term "blade shape" refers to the contour of the blade when you look at it from the side. There are a variety of basic shapes for practical folding knives, just as for other knives, and these basic shapes have numerous variations and hybrids.

Drop Point
Here the blade spine slightly slopes to form a tip, which generally sits in the upper third of the blade height. The cutting edge is more or less bulbous shaped. Despite distinct cutting properties, the tip remains robust and stable. The many variations of drop points are to a certain extent the all-in-one solution among knife blades. No other can be used as diversely and universally.

Spearpoint
The blade is similar to the drop point, but the tip is located almost on the center line. Very often, a spearpoint knife will have a more or less distinct swedge on the spine.

Clip Point
Also called a Bowie blade. The blade spine drops to the tip either in a straight line or in a concave curve. Sometimes,

Opposite: **Edge geometry (= cross section) and blade shape (= side profile) are essential for performance. (CRKT M40)**

5 | EDGY SHAPES: THE BLADES

THE PARTS OF THE BLADE

❶ **Swedge (false edge):** a part of the blade back that is often sharpened
❷ **Spine**
❸ **Blade face:** the unsharpened area below the spine
❹ **Ricasso:** the unsharpened base of the blade
❺ **Sharpening choil:** small indent at the start of the blade that aids sharpening with stones
❻ **Cutting edge (cutting bevel)**

Photos: CRKT, Kershaw

Ⓐ **Harpoon:** On some models the front area of the blade is widened. This widening then drops in a more or less sharp gradation toward the blade spine, which is optically similar to the barb of a harpoon. The gradation forms a rest for when the index finger or thumb is pressed on to the blade spine in order to exert more force.

Ⓑ **Ricasso with finger choil:** The choil is intended as a place to put the index finger. This special "front grip" (see page 72) allows for more control and greater exertion of force.

Ⓒ **Fuller:** This element has been borrowed from historical swords, for which it was, above all, intended to reduce weight. That is not so important for pocketknives. The fuller no longer has any real function but is now, above all, a design element.

the blade also has a sharpened swedge. Clip points have a very distinct tip that can be deployed with precision. However, the tips are sometimes very easily damaged.

Tanto

In this traditional Japanese knife shape, the tip is almost at the same height as the spine. The blade does not particularly taper either in width or thickness but then abruptly curves to the tip. The blade and, above all, the tip of the Tanto are very tough. This shape is frequently used when the knife is to withstand a lot.

American Tanto

In this shape, the cutting edge does not curve to the tip but has an angular edge that runs completely straight or almost completely straight to the tip. In American Tantos, you often find a combination of that grind on the tip and hollow grind on the cutting edge.

Reverse Tanto / K-tip

This shape became known as the reverse Tanto thanks to knife maker Warren Osborne, because it looks like an American Tanto turned on its head. This shape is also known as a K-tip. "K" stands for Kiritsuke; the blade tip is shape like these Japanese kitchen knives. K-tips are very versatile, and they allow for accurate and fine cuts.

Drop Point

Spearpoint

Clip Point

Tanto

American Tanto

Reverse Tanto / K-tip

Photos: Bestech, Cold Steel, CRKT, Spyderco

5 | EDGY SHAPES: THE BLADES

In some knives, the blade shape cannot be conclusively categorized as belonging to one classification. The Spyderco Tropen designed by knife maker Javier Vogt shows a pretty wild mixture.

EDGY SHAPES: THE BLADES | 5

Wharncliffe
This shape is traced back to the British nobleman Lord Wharncliffe, who is said to have invented it in the nineteenth century. We see a straight cutting edge. The spine slopes straight or with a convex curve into a distinct tip, which is exactly level with the cutting edge. The advantage is that the cutting edge always lies evenly on the material to be cut, and it can be used to make very powerful cuts.

Sheepfoot
With its predominantly straight edge, this shape is similar to the Wharncliffe blade, but in this case the tip is blunt and rounded and therefore only of limited use. You often find sheepfoot blades on rescue knives because it reduces the risk of injuring the accident victim when cutting them free.

Persian
This shape is derived from Asian blades. The cutting edge has a steep, bulbous, upward curve. It's highly effective in terms of cutting, but this extreme shape is not very versatile.

Hawkbill/Karambit
Hawkbill blades are more or less keenly curved, with an inwardly concave cutting edge, which allows very effective cuts with high transmission of force. It works very well when you need to cut something without anything underneath it; for example, ropes. Hawkbill blades are popular both as rescue knives and self-defense knives

Wharncliffe

Sheepfoot

Persian

Hawkbill/Karambit

Photos: Bestech, Cold Steel, Spyderco

Dagger

5 | EDGY SHAPES: THE BLADES

Photo: Spyderco

The recurve is a pronounced S-shaped curvature of the cutting edge. (Spyderco Hanan)

(karambits). They can only be used to a limited extent in daily life.

Dagger

This shape is symmetrical with a pointed tip. The blade spine is sharpened along the entire edge or at least heavily whetted. Dagger-shaped blades are primarily intended as weapons.

You call it a recurve when the cutting edge has a slight S shape. Apart from the elegant appearance, a recurve extends the length of the cutting edge in proportion to the blade length. The disadvantage is that a recurve is not easily sharpened using normal knife sharpeners. You can find recurve cutting edges on all presented types of blades, and that's why the recurve cutting edge is not its own blade shape classification.

THE EDGE GEOMETRY

To judge a blade, you need to first understand exactly what happens when making a cut. Unfortunately, at this point we are going to go a little into the theoretics and physics of blades. The most important factor for the cutting property is the cutting angle (wedge angle). Put simply, we should imagine the cross section of the blade as a triangle. The more pointed the triangle, the sharper the blade. And so, in theory, a knife blade should be as thin as possible to cut well. However, the thinner the blade, the lower the sideward toughness. Therefore, a compromise needs to be made.

When designing a knife blade, the objective is to give it a robust cross section with good cutting qualities. This cross section is called edge geometry. In order to talk about it, a few specialist terms need to be explained:

TERMS

- Blade thickness
- Blade spine
- Blade face
- Primary bevel
- Edge thickness
- Thickness
- Secondary bevel
- Cutting edge

98

THE "ZERO EDGE"

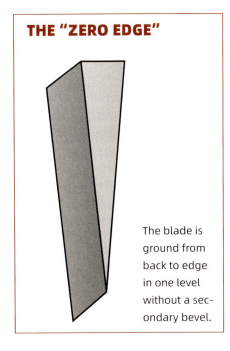

The blade is ground from back to edge in one level without a secondary bevel.

- Blade face: the unsharpened area below the spine
- Primary bevel: the part of the blade that leads into the secondary bevel
- Edge thickness: the maximal thickness of the secondary bevel at the transition to the primary bevel
- Secondary bevel: the sharply ground part of the blade
- Cutting edge: the outer edge

In many handcrafted knives, you can find a particularly good cutting edge geometry without a second bevel. Such a blade is ground to zero, as an expert would say. However, commercial knives produced in series are usually ground with a primary and secondary bevel. Such blades are not only considerably easier to produce, but also easier to resharpen.

A blade geometry with good cutting properties comes from the correct tapering of the blade geometry. It's an interplay of various factors, which interact with each other:

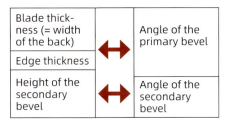

Regarding blade thickness, it's a question of what you value more: good cutting properties or as much stability as possible. Among other things, the blade thickness determines whether the primary bevel can be ground to a good cutting angle. While traditional designs, such as the Swiss pocketknife, rely on a thinner blade thickness of 2.5 mm (0.1 in.), over the years, 4 mm (0.16 in.) has become the conventional standard, and some manufacturers even go beyond that. A thickness between 3.0 and 3.5 mm (0.12 and 0.14 in.) is usually sufficient to lend the blade the necessary stability. At this thickness, it's still possible to achieve very good cutting properties.

Even more important than the blade is the thickness of the secondary bevel at the transition point to the primary bevel. It's also known as "behind-the-edge thickness" or just "edge thickness." The interplay between the angle of the primary bevel, the cutting edge bevel thickness, and the

5 | EDGY SHAPES: THE BLADES

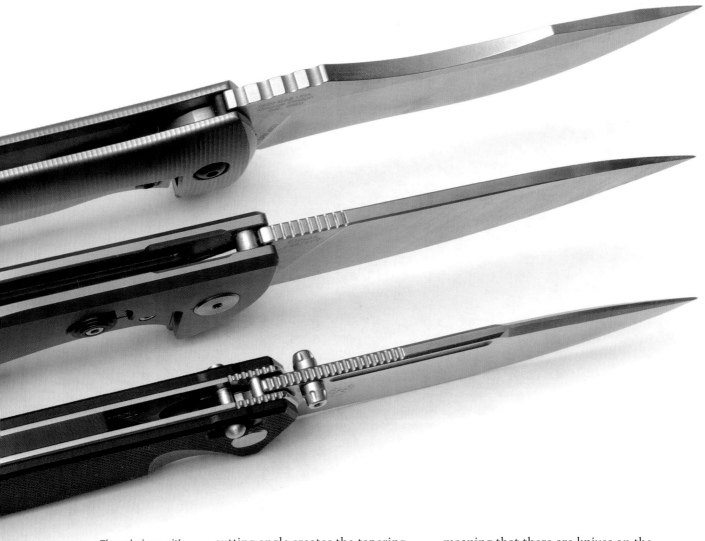

Three knives with different blade thicknesses (0.16-, 0.14-, and 0.12-inch) and different cutting properties

cutting angle creates the tapering.

If the secondary bevel is too thick and its angle too wide, it creates poor tapering: at the transition between the bevels, a noticeable shoulder is formed, as the knife makers call it. For pocketknives, the rule of thumb goes that the secondary bevel thickness should not be more than 0.19–0.023 inch.

Unfortunately, even renowned knife brands do not always manage to create a blade geometry that cuts well, meaning that there are knives on the market with very differing cutting properties. If the aforementioned factors are not correct, then although the secondary bevel is sharp and can even slice cleanly through paper, the cutting properties as a whole remain mediocre. The graphic on page 102 shows three different taperings, of which only one performs really well.

The cutting bevel thickness can be properly measured only with calipers.

SHARPENING ANGLES

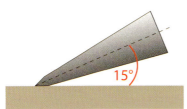

The grinding angle is always half the cutting angle. For a cutting angle of 30°, it needs to be ground at 15° on both sides.

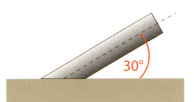

Using a one-sided chisel grind, the sharpening angle is the same as the cutting angle.

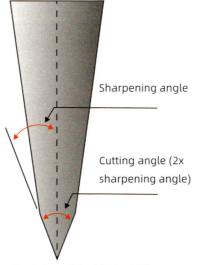

Front view of the blade: With a symmetrically sharpened blade, the cutting angle is the sum of both sharpening angles.

Of course, not every knife enthusiast has such a measuring device at home. In addition, the precise measurement of the secondary bevel thickness is not easy. However, by using a small trick you can get a good impression of the blade geometry. Take the blade between your thumb and index finger, holding on to the blade face. Press your finger and thumb gently together and pull the blade from your fingers slightly diagonally to the cutting edge.

Repeat the process two or three times. In this way you get a good impression of whether it benefits from good tapering with a gentle transition between the bevels, or if the secondary bevel thickness is very broad and the shoulders are clearly noticeable. If you are still uncertain, you can compare it with a thin ground pairing knife from the kitchen: they usually have a blade that cuts very well with extreme tapering, thin secondary bevel thickness, and gentle transition to the secondary bevel.

5 | EDGY SHAPES: THE BLADES

BLADE GEOMETRY IN COMPARISON

The properties of a blade depend on the interaction between the grinding angle of the primary and secondary bevel, as well as the thickness of the secondary bevel. In the example, a blade with the same thickness of 4.0 mm (0.16 in.) and height of 2.5 cm (1 in.) has been sharpened using three different geometries from the spine to the start of the secondary bevel.

Very robust blade geometry (left): The primary bevel narrows to a secondary bevel thickness of 0.8 mm (0.031 in.); the secondary bevel is ground to a 50° angle. Thanks to the abrupt transition from a broad secondary bevel thickness to a wide angle, distinct shoulders are formed. These measurements create very robust cutting edges, but not good cutting qualities.

Moderate blade geometry (center): The primary bevel narrows to a secondary bevel thickness of 0.5 mm (0.019 in.), and the adjoining secondary bevel is ground to a 40° angle. Although the shoulders are distinct, they are moderate. With sufficient stability, the cutting properties are very respectable.

Good blade geometry for cutting (right): The primary bevel narrows to a secondary bevel thickness of just 0.3 mm (0.012 in.), and the adjoining secondary bevel is ground to a sharp 30° angle. There is a gentle transition between the bevels, without any noticeable shoulders. The cutting properties are good to very good. As a result, the stability of the cutting edge is not very high when force is exerted from the side.

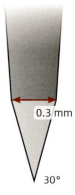

For a blade to cut well, it must be sharp. If a knife is blunt, then the cutting edge becomes more or less rounded through use. To sharpen, the secondary cutting bevel is ground until it narrows to a sharp cutting edge.

Upon very heavy use and regular sharpening, a noticeable material stripping occurs on the secondary bevel. As a result, the secondary bevel moves farther up the blade, meaning both that the behind-the-edge thickness becomes increasingly wider and the shoulders become increasingly broader. The edge geometry worsens. Therefore, you need to grind the secondary bevel at a slightly sharper angle to make up for it.

EDGY SHAPES: THE BLADES | 5

EFFECT OF THE KNIFE'S SHARPNESS

Sharp blade: Cutting pressure is exerted on a small surface.

Blunt blade: Cutting pressure is distributed over a larger area.

The sharper the wedge, the lower the force.

A question of thickness: The narrower the cutting edge is, the less force is necessary to separate the fibers of the material to be cut.

The tapering of the edge geometry as well as the form of the shoulders can be felt between your thumb and index finger.

5 | EDGY SHAPES: THE BLADES

A sharpened, cleanly polished cutting edge can even cut a piece of paper held in the air.

From the side view, the secondary cutting bevel becomes broader as a result. Eventually, the adjusted grinding angle for the secondary bevel is no longer enough, and regrinding the primary bevel cannot be avoided. However, until that stage, a lot of wear and tear has happened and that only really happens to intensively used work knives.

If you run your thumb over the cutting edge of a knife straight from the factory, you can sometimes feel a very slightly rough cutting edge, even though the blade is sharp and cuts well. It's a microserration, which occurs when the secondary bevel has been ground but not polished afterward. The cross section is a little untidy, but that is not really noticeable during normal cutting work. In contrast, if you can feel very rough areas or bumps on the secondary bevel ex-works, then that is a manufacturing defect. On a high-quality knife, the secondary bevel is polished and sharp so that it gives a clean, really smooth cut.

SHARPENING

The red area is removed.

By sharpening the side surfaces, the blunted cutting edge becomes pointed and sharp again.

SERRATIONS

Serrations have been seen on bread or steak knives for a long time. But it was only with the tactical folding knife that it was introduced to the world of pocketknives. The pointed teeth can quickly cut through very tough and resistant materials. Typical uses include cutting safety belts or synthetic ropes. Serrations are found mainly on rescue knives or models that are intended for the police, the military, or other such services. Generally, it's only the back part of the blade that is equipped with serrations. There are only a few brands that produce knives with fully serrated blades.

For normal cutting work, the serrations are more of a hinderance. The cut that a serrated blade makes is not smooth or neat because it "rips" rather than cuts. A further problem is that a serrated blade is difficult to resharpen. To do so, you need special conically shaped grinding equipment to bore into the "valleys." However, the advantage is that a serrated blade remains sharp for a long time because it's primarily the tips the become worn, while the small concave cutting edges don't wear as much. Regarding the shape of the serrations, there are many variations that range from very pointed and aggressive sawtooth edges to gently rounded waves. Also, the sequence and size of the valleys are very different. In this regard, each knife brand follows their own recipe. Knife enthusiasts can frequently tell the manufacturer of the knife on the basis of the shape of the serrations.

Photo: Buck

Many knives have serrations on half of the blade.

You often find serrations on rescue knives.

Photo: Spyderco

THE GRIND TYPES

The biggest difference regarding the various blade geometries is primarily found in the grind type. For pocketknives there are six basic types:

Flat Grind (V-grind)
The blade is ground from the back to the secondary bevel, almost like a large wedge. It provides a good mix of stability and cutting properties.

Saber Grind
A large area under the blade spine is not ground at all. The grinding only begins afterward, so that the secondary bevel has a fairly steep angle. This blade geometry is used, above all, when the most robust blade is desired. The specific American term "saber grind" has also spread in Germany, so now it's referred to as "Säbelschliff."

Hollow Saber Grind
If you want the blade spine to be as strong as possible without impairing the cutting properties, the secondary bevel is ground to be hollow (concave). If this is done properly, it gives a thinner angle that cuts better. A further advantage for the user: these blades can be relatively easily and quickly resharpened. However, the hollow saber grind is really exacting to grind. If it's not done properly, the transition between the primary and secondary bevel is so thick that despite the hollow grind, the angle of the secondary bevel is too wide.

Scandi Grind
The Scandi grind forms an exception from blade geometry with secondary and primary bevels and originated on Nordic knives. On Scandi grind knives, there is only one bevel after the blade face, which is ground in a straight profile to point at the cutting edge. When resharpening, you have to grind the whole primary bevel, which causes considerable work and is a reason why a few manufacturers cheat and grind a small auxiliary bevel on the cutting edge. A Scandi grind pocketknife is extremely rare.

Convex Grind
This grind is very rare among industrially produced knives because it's very laborious. The German word *ballig* means that the blade surface slightly convexly curves outwardly. Generally, it's ground straight to the tip or there is only a minimal cutting bevel. The big advantage of the convex grind is that it combines great cutting ability with a high level of stability. The disadvantage is that to sharpen it correctly requires skill or special tricks.

Chisel Grind
This geometry is called "Beitelschliff," because just like a Stechbeitel (ripping chisel), only one side of the blade is ground. The theory behind the chisel grind is that the blade becomes more tough (thanks to more mass) and is also easier to resharpen because you

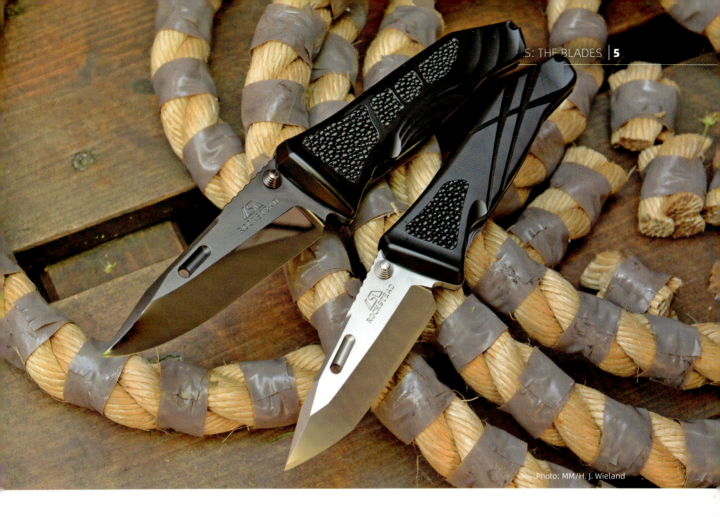

TYPES OF GRIND

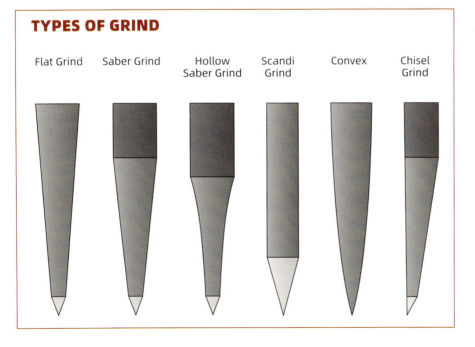

Flat Grind　　Saber Grind　　Hollow Saber Grind　　Scandi Grind　　Convex　　Chisel Grind

Just like the Higo, most knives by Rockstead are slightly convex as well as ground straight to a point, and they cut fantastically well.

5 | EDGY SHAPES: THE BLADES

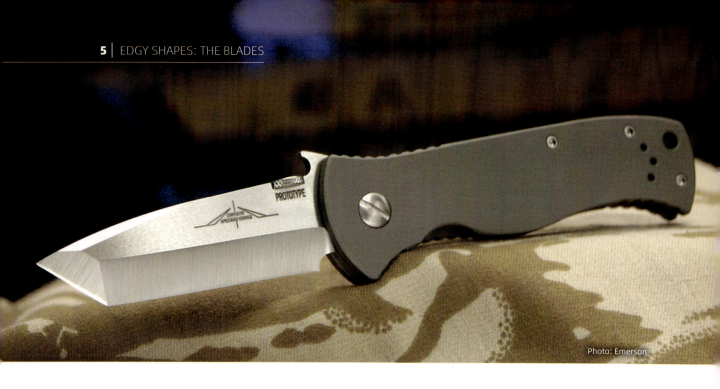

Emerson CQC-7 with full one-sided chisel grind. When ground on this side, only left-handers can use it without problems.

only need to work on one side. Emerson Knives is a company specializing in producing knives with chisel grinds.

The concept behind it isn't exactly new: such one-sided grinds are also found on Japanese cooking knives. However, the Japanese knifesmiths know that for this grind, you need to differentiate between right- and left-handers. As a result of the one-sided grind, the blade veers to one side of the material when cutting. If the grind is on the correct side—namely, the outer side of the hand—then this effect is neutralized by the natural body mechanics.

However, if the grind is on the wrong side, it's practically impossible to make a straight and neat cut, no matter how hard you concentrate on countering it with your hand.

For Japanese cooking knives ground on one side, there are models for right- and left-handers. For optical reasons, chisel grinds on pocketknives are always on the "show side" of the knife, where the company logo is shown. Even Emerson states that the chisel grind is ground on the left side as a "visual distinguishing characteristic." In fact, all chisel grind pocketknives available on the market are therefore ground for left-handers.

Combi Grind

Sometimes, attempts are made to combine two different blade geometries with each other, and in doing so, to get the best of both worlds. Regarding these combi grinds, there are two different concepts: very often the area around the tip is ground to have a stronger blade geometry, so that the tip is less likely to break. Sometimes, the back part of the blade is also made to be more robust, so that you can carry out vigorous cutting and carving work with this area. A moderate version of such a combi grind is often found on the American

EDGY SHAPES: THE BLADES | 5

Photo: CRKT

Tanto: the slanted blade tip is ground flat while the rest of the blade is hollow.

With the CRKT BT-70, the blade is ground in two different directions, almost half-half.

EMERSON'S "V-GRIND"

The chisel grind became popular above all thanks to the tactical folding knives by Ernest Emerson. If you don't want a chisel grind but value the other characteristics of Emerson knives (e.g., the excellent hand comfort), buy a model with the so-called V-grind.

Ernest Emerson's V-grind is not a normal flat grind. Instead, the secondary bevel has only been ground on the left side, which they call a chisel edge at Emerson. These blades do not veer so severely to the side, whereas a real chisel grind does; however, straight and accurate cuts are also more difficult with it.

SPEED AND FORCE

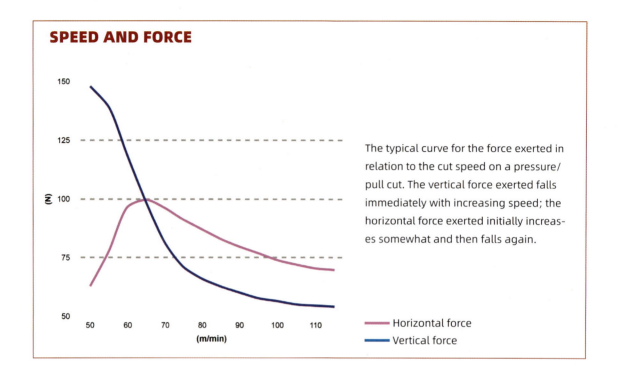

The typical curve for the force exerted in relation to the cut speed on a pressure/pull cut. The vertical force exerted falls immediately with increasing speed; the horizontal force exerted initially increases somewhat and then falls again.

DYNAMIC EDGE ANGLE

Through the cutting movement, the previously static cutting angle becomes dynamic and changes. The faster the movement, the sharper the angle.

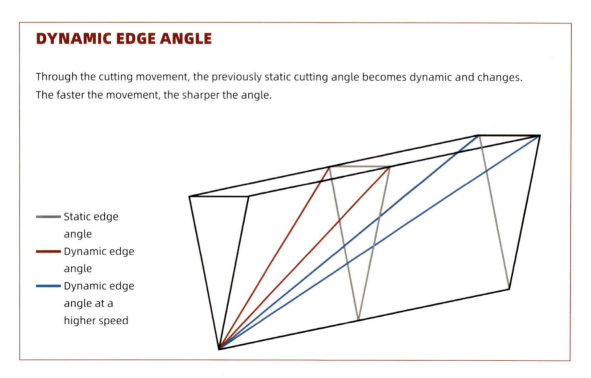

— Static edge angle
— Dynamic edge angle
— Dynamic edge angle at a higher speed

Photo: CRKT

THE IDEAL BLADE LENGTH

When working with a knife, you nearly always use the combined pressure/pull cut: the hand presses the blade on the material to be cut and at the same time makes a pulling or pushing movement. Laboratory readings have shown that with increasing cutting speed, both the vertical and horizontal exertion of force reduces when cutting.

It's down to the so-called dynamic edge angle. Through the cutting movement, the edge angle becomes sharper in terms of physics. And the faster the cutting movement, the sharper the edge angle becomes (and therefore better at cutting).*

What is often missed in the description of the edge geometry is the human factor: body mechanics and acceleration distance. We all know that you have to travel a certain distance in order to reach top speed. That also goes for arm movements. Transferred to the knife, that means that with a very short knife, the cutting movement from blade base to the top has often already ended before you have reached the top speed.

---

*You can read about this in more detail in the book *Messerklingen und Stahl* (*Knife Blades and Steel*) by Roman Landes.

In addition to the sharpness of the secondary bevel, the angles of the blade geometry are crucial for the cutting properties.

HOW TO PROPERLY MEASURE BLADE LENGTH

Depending on the method of measuring, you can get different values for the blade length. Blade length becomes relevant mainly when it's to be determined whether a knife is restricted by law. Therefore, it's important to use the same measuring method as the police and the justice authorities. Generally, in Germany, the blade length is measured "from the top of the blade in a straight line to the point where the handle intersects the line," as the German Federal Criminal Police Office (Bundeskriminalamt) explains. When in doubt, don't measure "the maximum length extending from the handle but, rather, only the length that would be effective in a straight stab . . ." as stated on an info sheet from the Bayerische Landeskriminalamt (Bavarian Criminal Police Office): "The effective blade length is measured from the blade tip to the front border of the handle (hand protection)." The measuring method of the effective blade length (*top image*) was also confirmed by the German Federal Criminal Police Office, since, "if applicable, a knife can only penetrate up to the very front of the handle." Therefore, police jargon often refers to "penetration depth" for the effective blade length. You cannot always rely on the measurements stated in catalogs, in particular regarding knives from China. Many importers simply accept the manufacturer's technical data without measuring it themselves. However, according to the Chinese law, only the cutting edge length (i.e., the sharp ground part of the blade) counts. Depending on how big the ricasso is, there is sometimes a significant difference between the catalog measurements and the legal blade length.

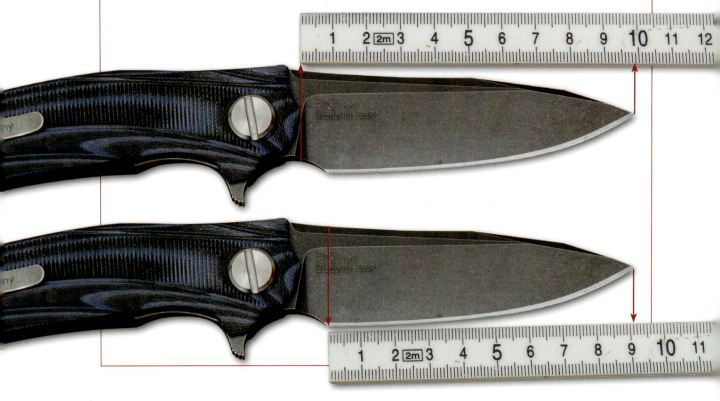

Photo: Chris Reeve

That inevitably means that the shorter the blade and therefore the shorter the acceleration distance, the slower the cutting movement and the less advantage you gain from the dynamic edge angle. In contrast with a longer blade, you can cut faster, meaning that the effective cutting angle becomes sharper.

Put simply: the longer the blade, the more effective the cutting action. That is one of several reasons that professional cooks use large cooking knives with a blade length of 20 cm or more. In practice, the limits for the blade length are determined by how it's used, in particular for pocketknives, which have to be folded together and carried. These factors give a general rule of thumb for a good blade length: as compact as necessary, but as long as possible.

There are some pocketknives with blades of 11 cm or more on the market. However, most large folding knives are no longer than 10 cm (4 inches). That corresponds to a handle length of about 13 cm (5.1 in.). This size plus a clip can still be comfortably carried in the trouser pocket.

Even if a large pocketknife with a 10 cm blade is practical in terms of functionality, there are of course good reasons to prefer more-compact models; for example, national laws about carrying weapons. Or sometimes, your social circle may be a factor, because a large pocketknife may attract critical looks.

Most practical folding knives are between 7 and 9 cm (2.57 and 3.54 in.) long. Due to the international focus of the large knife producers, 8.9 cm (3.5 inches) is a very widespread length. To accommodate the different markets, tastes, and requirements, many companies offer their popular models in several sizes.

The Sebenza by Chris Reeve is available with a blade length of 9.1 or 7.6 cm (3.6 or 3 in.).

5 | EDGY SHAPES: THE BLADES

The two models of the CRKT Pharaco cater to different approaches. The blade has been ground at different angles and is also partially serrated.

Photo: CRKT

EDGY SHAPES: THE BLADES | **5**

115

Photo: Sharp by Coop

CHAPTER 6
FOR SAFETY'S SAKE: LOCKING SYSTEMS

Every knife enthusiast who's cut themselves by accidentally closing the blade while working with a slip-joint pocketknife absolutely knows that a locking system on a pocketknife is an important safety factor. However, knife enthusiasts passionately discuss the question of how tough a locking system should be and which of the many systems on the market is the best.

Some people believe that a locking system should be as tough as possible, and all other functions should be deemed less important. Others are of the opinion that the locking systems in daily practice should be a practical compromise between toughness and comfort of use, naturally without seriously neglecting the safety aspect. "You buy a car because of its 1,000 horsepower, but you like it because it's comfortable and reliable," says knife maker Flavio Ikoma, the inventor of the deadbolt-lock (which will be presented later).

A particularly important aspect is one-handed use. While knives with

"The shifts of fortune text the reliability of friends."

–Cicero -

liner, frame, axis, or button locks can be easily unlocked and closed with one hand, it does not work as easily and smoothly with other systems.

New locking systems for pocketknives keep coming onto the market. Some are relatively short lived, while others are used for decades and are tried and tested. In this chapter, I do not intend to provide a full overview (that would make for a very long book), but I will explain the most important systems on the market. The most focus will be placed on the liner lock. It's by far the most important locking system on the market.

Opposite: Titanium folding knife by knife maker Tyler Turner. Frame locks are becoming increasingly more popular with titanium handles.

TESTING LOCKING SYSTEMS

Many of us have seen the ruthless YouTube test videos by Cold Steel. The manufacturer does all kinds of things to demonstrate the cutting effect of its knives and the toughness of the Tri-Ad-Lock system. For example, a whole motor block or even several hundred pounds in the form of weight plates are attached to the handle of a pocketknife. Other tests measure the holding force of the locking systems by using electronically controlled winders. If you google "knife lock tests," you will also find many other, more or less sensible test methods. Many are not recommended. However, there are some good methods for home use.

If you've just bought a knife, it makes sense to check the locking system. It's fairly easy to do; first, you open the knife, vigorously jiggle the opened blade, and check whether the blade has any vertical or sideways slackness and whether it locks securely. If the blade is already wobbling up and down or sideways in the handle, then something isn't right.

Then turn the opened knife so the spine is facing down, place the front area of the blade on a firm base, and exercise increasing force on it. When doing so, ensure that your fingers aren't in the way of the blade, possibly folding inward on them. It's important that pressure is placed as far to the point of hte blade as possible, because the lever action it makes has a particularly strong effect. The third test is relatively brutal; the spinewack test is carried out from the same hand position but without permanent pressure. Instead, the blade spine is hit with force several times against a base. If you are considering returning the knife because of a defective locking system, it's best to put a newspaper over the base so that the blade does not get scratched.

In the photos below, we didn't use any paper protection to show the nicks in the wooden base from hitting it.

Attention: To avoid injuries, always keep your fingers out of the blade's trajectory or wear cut-resistant gloves or—even better—do both!

Elegant folding knives by Michael Walker, the inventor of the liner lock

THE LINER LOCK

The liner lock is the most widespread locking system. There are two main reasons for its popularity. First, it's very easy and comfortable to use with one hand, and it was exactly for that reason that it was developed. You don't need to exercise any force to open a liner lock. And it can even be easily closed with one hand. To do so, you only need to push the locking flat spring to the side with your thumb.

Second, a liner lock is affordable and easy to produce because, in contrast to other systems, it doesn't need many additional components. However, an awful lot can go wrong in its production. That's why the liner lock has a reputation for a certain unreliability.

Today's liner lock system stems from the US knife maker Micheal Walker. After various experiments with slip joints and back lock knives, in 1980, Walker tinkered around with a new locking system to create a pocketknife with new properties:

- It should be as easy as possible to open and close with one hand, and it should be possible to do so without having to change the position of the knife in the hand.
- Wear and tear that occurs over time should be accommodated.
- The "gap" on the tang, inherent in all back lock knives back then and whose sharp edge can destroy trouser pockets, was to disappear.

6 | FOR SAFETY'S SAKE: LOCKING SYSTEMS

The liner lock is very simple to use and very easy to manufacture.

Photo: CRKT

Michael Walker's liner lock met all these requirements and since then has been a worldwide success. As its base, Walker used a system that already existed at the turn of the century, but he significantly improved it. One of the important changes was the ball detent, which is a small ball pressed into the flat spring, which keeps the folded-in blade safely in the handle. Another positive effect is that in contrast to back lock knives, the liner lock allows the back of the handle to be partially open so that it's easier to clean the inside of the knife.

There are two main types of liner lock. In most commercially available models, the flat spring is produced as part of the liner itself (locking liner). For self-supporting handles, it's made as its own component and positioned inside the handle scales, where it's screwed into a milled groove (nested liner).

The basic principles of both models are the same: the flat spring the blade axis, and the stop pin (blade stopper) create a power triangle. The blade is locked between the flat spring and the stop pin.

For optimal functioning, it's very important that the contact point between the flat spring and the tang is

THE POWER TRIANGLE

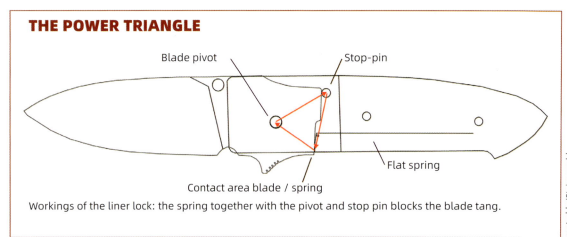

Workings of the liner lock: the spring together with the pivot and stop pin blocks the blade tang.

Fronteddu/Steigerwald

120

as far as possible from the blade pivot. In that way, it generates the correct amount of force so that the lever force does not overload it. Ideally, the power triangle is an equilateral triangle (with sides of equal length) with three 60° angles, since it's the strongest geometric form. However, in knife construction this exact shape is only rarely achieved. The flat spring is shaped at the front so that only a small area of a few millimeters comes into contact with the tang. As a result, the spring pressure is more concentrated in this small area.

The locking liner is normally around 1.5 mm (0.06 in.) thick. You can also find thicknesses of 2 mm (0.08 in.) in particularly robust knives. The liners are either made of steel or, in the case of high-quality knives, titanium. Titanium is often regarded as the ideal material for liner locks: upon contact with steel, there is noticeable friction. You have the feeling that the titanium spring bar sticks to the tang. However, sometimes this sticking effect is so forceful that it's very difficult to unlatch the blade. One of the most frequent causes of this problem is the

> **IMPORTANT DETAILS**
>
> Here the spring is not in contact with the blade tang.
>
> Contact is not even but dotted (approximately 1. in.).
>
> The front end of the flat spring is shaped so that the force is concentrated on smaller areas.

Diagram: Fronteddu/Steigerwald

The flat spring should lock as soon as possible (i.e., in the first one-third of the ramp of the tang).

Photo: CRKT

6 | FOR SAFETY'S SAKE: LOCKING SYSTEMS

THE DETENT BALL

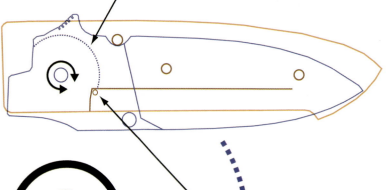

Grind marks from the detent ball on the blade tang

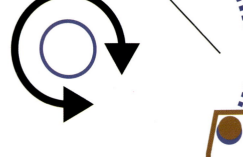

The indent for the detent ball in the blade is drilled approximately 0.5 mm (0.02 in.) after the end of the grind marks.

Through the insertion of the ball, the spring becomes somewhat headed. That should be considered when manufacturing the knife.

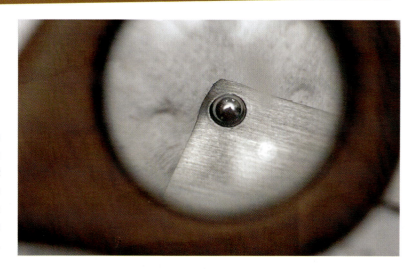

Photo and Diagram: Fronteddu/Steigerwald

incorrect (too broad) angle of the tang ramp (more on this soon). If a titanium locking liner jams, then graphite helps; use a pencil to lightly cover the contact areas on the tang.

If a liner lock has been correctly designed, then wear and tear from using it is accommodated. The tang forms a diagonal ramp. When just out of the factory, the spring bar should lock as soon as possible (i.e., on the outer edge of this ramp). With increasing use, the spring may move farther along the ramp. If, in factory condition, a flat spring already locks late (i.e., only in the center or back of the ramp), then the liner lock has not been manufactured correctly. A very common cause of this error is an incorrect angle of the blade ramp (see image on next page).

With increasing wear and tear on the spring, the friction and contact area with the tang become bigger. As a result, the wear and tear will slow down. In particular, knives with heavy blades and titanium liners show noticeable wear over time. Eventually, you end up with a radial blade slackness, and the locking system no longer functions reliably. That is caused by usage (e.g., very frequent and forceful flicking open) or too-soft titanium.

In fact, only hardenable 6Al$_4$V should be used for the spring bar. As Bob Terzuola explained, wear and tear reduce after the wearing-in phase for titanium 6Al$_4$V because, in the locking area, the titanium becomes work

hardened. However, for reasons of cost, softer and more-malleable titanium alloys are sometimes used; admittedly these locking liners noticeably wear. Therefore, for liner lock knives (and not only for these ones), you should avoid forcefully flicking open the blade with wide swinging motions.

In the case of normal and regular use of the knife, it takes several years until the flat spring has been worn down so much that it's right at the back end of the ramp. And even then, it still locks reliably. If that should no longer be the case, there is only one thing to do: remove the locking liner and stretch it somewhat with a few taps of the hammer. However, you should get that done by an expert, such as a knife maker with liner lock experience.

Liner locks and frame locks work according to the same principles.

6 | FOR SAFETY'S SAKE: LOCKING SYSTEMS

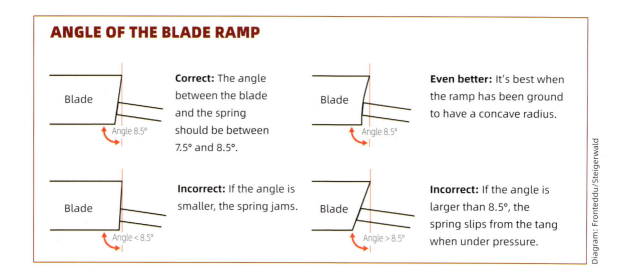

Diagram: Fronteddu/Steigerwald

For an additional safety lock, a block is positioned between the spring and the handle scales.

Photo: CRKT

Yet, it's only worth such effort for high-quality knives or well-loved treasures.

The detent ball is a further important factor in the correct functioning of liner locks. This small ball made of steel, or ceramic on high-quality knives, sits on the inside on the front of the flat spring When the knife is closed, the detent balls fit perfectly in a recess in the blade tang. The retention force created as a result prevents the knife from accidentally opening in trouser pockets, which is important especially for knives that are carried tip up. The detent ball also has an effect on the blade movement: when folding the knife, it means that over a few millimeters the blade is pulled inward by the force of the detent ball.

If the detent ball latches too securely in the slot in the tang, you need a lot of force to overcome this resistance when opening the knife, so that the blade goes from initially not moving to suddenly opening with high energy. This phenomenon can happen when the recess in the tang is too deep or the tension of the flat spring is too high. Sometimes, on a brand-new, affordable knife you may hear a slight scraping when opening it—that is the tang moving over the detent ball. Some oil helps, and after some time playing around with it, the mechanism is broken in. If the

FOR SAFETY'S SAKE: LOCKING SYSTEMS | 6

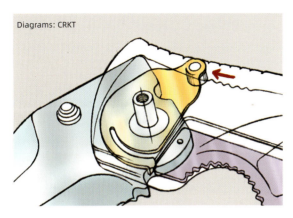
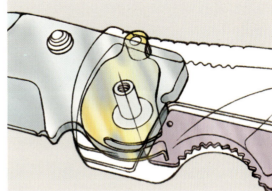

Diagrams: CRKT

With a small slider on the top of the handle, the LAWKS back-up safety systems are activated.

sound is very loud and does not go away, then it's a manufacturing defect.

In the knife community, you hear of failed liner locks often. The reasons for this are mistakes in the design and production. One possible source of the defect is that the flat spring has not been sufficiently bent. You can repair it yourself, by carefully further bending the flat spring. However, far more frequently the ramp on the tang has been ground incorrectly. For the liner lock to work properly, the ramp requires the correct gradient angle. As a rule, it's between 7.5 and 8.5°, with a maximum tolerance range of 7 to 9°.* With a clearly smaller angle, the flat spring jams very frequently, and you often only succeed in unlocking the blade with a coin or, in a worst-case scenario, with a screwdriver.

It's even worse when the angle is too broad, because it presents the danger that the flat spring will slip from the ramp and the locking system will fail. For series knives produced in large quantities, it's often not just an individual knife with the problem but a whole batch that has been incorrectly manufactured. Until just a few years ago, it occurred relatively frequently, but it has now become significantly rarer. However, a high purchase price and a renowned brand do not always protect you against such cases.

In the experience of Bob Terzuola and other knife makers such as Stefan Steigerwald, the best method for a liner lock is to grind the ramp at a slightly concave angle of 8.5°. It means that toward the end of the ramp, it becomes increasingly steep, which in turn better accommodates wear on the flat spring. For industrially produced knives, a concave ground ramp is usually only found on high-quality knives from prestigious brands.

---

* If you would like further information, I recommend the book *Liner Lock Knives* by Stefan Steigerwald and Peter Fronteddu.

125

6 | FOR SAFETY'S SAKE: LOCKING SYSTEMS

The frame lock is somewhat more tough than the liner lock. Otherwise, the main difference is its appearance.

It's important for the functioning of the liner lock that the spring action of the leaf spring is neither too weak nor too strong. In its closed state, the flat spring is also pressing sideways against the blade. If this pressure becomes too strong, then the blade does not sit straight in the handle, and it doesn't really move smoothly. In the worst case, it's pushed against the other liner and scrapes it every time it's opened and closed. In that case, you need to adjust the blade motion (see page 159). If that does not help, the only option is to slightly bend the spring back.

It's very comfortable to use the liner lock. However, in contrast to the back lock, where the unlocking lever is positioned on the outside of the knife and is easily accessible, you need to be on the inside of the knife to lock it. Depending on the knife design, unlocking it may be difficult, in particular when the liner lies flush with the handle scales. For this reason, it was commonplace especially in the 1980s and the early 1990s to include a recess in the front handle scales, which left part of the spring exposed. Apart from the fact that many knife enthusiasts think such a recess is ugly, there were frequent safety considerations; for example, the fear that if you held the knife tightly, you could accidently unlock it. Therefore, knife makers and producers have come up with various solutions.

One of the simplest solutions to make the locking liner more grippy is to add anti-slip serration on its underside to allow the thumb to find hold

126

When using light titanium, you can make the spring stronger and more tough, as in this example by knife maker Sean O'Hare.

when the liner is otherwise flush with the underside of the handle. Another practice is to reduce the width of the handle by 1–2 mm (0.04–0.08 in.) in the relevant place, so that although there is no large recess, the flat spring still slightly protrudes. That's usually combined with additional anti-slip serration.

As you can see, there are many aspects to consider when producing a liner lock. As a manufacturer, you can get a lot wrong. However, there are reasons why the system is the world's most popular locking system for pocketknives (e.g., the operation is as easy as it's comfortable), and a well-constructed and accurately made liner lock is a safe locking system.

Many knife producers, above in the affordable-knives category, still insert back-up safety systems in their liner lock models. It's essentially based on using a small slider to push a bar in front of the locked leaf spring so that the spring can no longer slip outward off the ramp. One of the first of these systems was developed by knife makers Ron Lake and Michael Walker. It was the LAWKS (Lake and Walker Knife Safety), which is used in many CRKT knives. These days, there are various other additional back-up safety systems which are based on a similar principle.

The biggest criticism of such safety systems is that, in practice, you may forget the additional step or simply not do it out of convenience. At the start of 2006, CRKT reacted with the introduction of the AutoLAWKS. The

6 | FOR SAFETY'S SAKE: LOCKING SYSTEMS

LEFT-HANDERS AND LOCKING SYSTEMS

You can tell by the locking system; what knives are really suitable for left-handers. Back locks, tri-ad locks, axis locks, etc. are designed so that they can be used easily on both sides. Even the compression lock can, with a bit of practice, be used by both right-handers and left-handers. In contrast, liner locks, frame locks, button locks, and even deadbolt locks only allow true one-handed operation from one side. These knives are made for right-handers. Knife makers can of course design models specially for left-handers by making a full mirror image of the handle design, such as this model by Keith Ouye. However, these knives are almost never found in series production.

Photo: Sharp by Coop

functionality is the same as with LAWKS, but the slider is equipped with a spring. When the knife opens, the block is automatically pushed forward. AutoLAWKS knives are somewhat more difficult to close than the standard LAWKS models, but it's possible with one hand. Although the system is still being made today, CRKT no longer uses the name LAWKS.

THE FRAME LOCK

The frame lock is a close relative to the liner lock. It's based on the same principles of physics and is used in the same manner. The difference is that in this instance the bakc-up safety systems are not part of the liner but is part of the handle frame itself, which is made of steel or titanium.

The frame lock became famous primarily thanks to the Sebenza by Chris Reeve, who is considered to be the inventor of this locking mechanism. Brought onto the market in 1991, the Sebenza, which at the time was still made by hand, became a success story. At the time, it was one of the few knives whose handle was made completely of titanium. Chris Reeve described the locking system as an integral lock, and it's still called that at Chris Reeve Knives. However, in the knife world, the name "frame lock" has become established.

Thanks to modern, computer-controlled milling technology, the frame lock has become very popular in recent years because makers can sell elaborately worked titanium handles at affordable prices. Be it steel or titanium, the design of a frame lock remains the same. On the locking side of the handle, a slit is incorporated so that a spring bar is created. At the back end of the flat spring, the material is thinned so that the spring becomes movable. At 3-4 mm (0.12-0.16 in.) thick, this flat spring clearly has a larger material thickness than the spring bar in a liner lock, which also makes it more tough. Due to its thickness, the spring of a frame lock is referred to as a "lock bar." Furthermore, this lock bar

The Sebenza by Chris Reeve was the first knife with a frame lock.

Photo: Chris Reeve

Photos: Sharp by Coop

FOR SAFETY'S SAKE: LOCKING SYSTEMS | 6

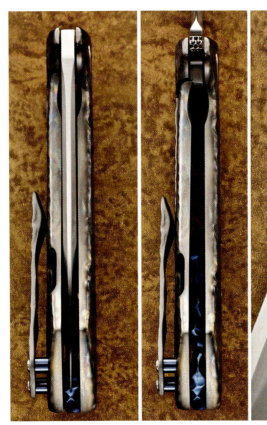

is usually pushed inward by hand when using it, which results in the closing force also being increased.

Since the frame lock works according to the same mechanical principles as a liner lock, you have to be mindful of the same factors:

- the detent ball
- the power triangle between the blade pivot, stop pin, and lock bar
- the correct distance between the lock bar and the blade pivot
- the correct angle of the ramp
- the correct bend of the spring

However, there are also factors that are different from a liner lock. For example, when unlocking the frame lock there is the risk that the spring bar is pushed too far out and, as a result, overtravel—meaning that afterward the locking system no longer functions. To prevent that, an overtravel stop can be integrated. Trailblazing in this regard was knife maker Rick Hinderer, who screwed a small disk on the outside and called the whole thing a lock bar stabilizer. Depending on the design of the handle, an external disk may drastically distract the knife's appearance.

Blade position, frame lock alignment, stop pin construction, etc.: Singularity by knife maker Todd Rexford shows everything that needs to be considered in the design.

6 | FOR SAFETY'S SAKE: LOCKING SYSTEMS

The manufacturing quality of a frame lock can be easily recognized by the width of the lock bar's slit.

On the Zero Tolerance 0562 and Defcon TD 1001, a disk on the frame protects the lock bar from overtraveling to the outside.

Photo: Sharp by Coop

With the bolster lock, most of the lock bar is hidden from sight by the handle scales (custom folding knife by Jonathan McNees).

Therefore, nowadays most manufacturers have brought the overtravel stop inside the knife. It's screwed to the lock bar and is blocked by the handle scales. Usually, an internal overtravel stop can barely be seen.

With the frame lock, the lock bar, milled out of the handle, is visible on the back of the knife. Therefore, some knife enthusiasts don't like it for aesthetic reasons. However, for most knife fans, it's crucial how wide the slit between the lock bar and the rest of the handle has been made. On high-end frame locks, there is generally a gap of less than 1 mm; however, on cheaper models the gap is frequently over 2 mm and as a result is really ugly.

A solution for the aesthetic problem is a type of frame lock that is known as the bolster lock. Its handle is designed so that the majority of the frame lock is hidden by the screwed-on handle scales. The locking system is then only visible on the bolster of the knife. A special variation of the frame lock system is known as the subframe lock, where a locking liner is positioned in the handle scales that moves up to the stop and protrudes over a few centimeters from a recess in the handle scales. However, if the knife also has a thumb blade lifter, it's possible that upon opening the knife, the subframe lock and the detent ball are pressed involuntarily into the tang, meaning that opening the knife is constricted.

6 | FOR SAFETY'S SAKE: LOCKING SYSTEMS

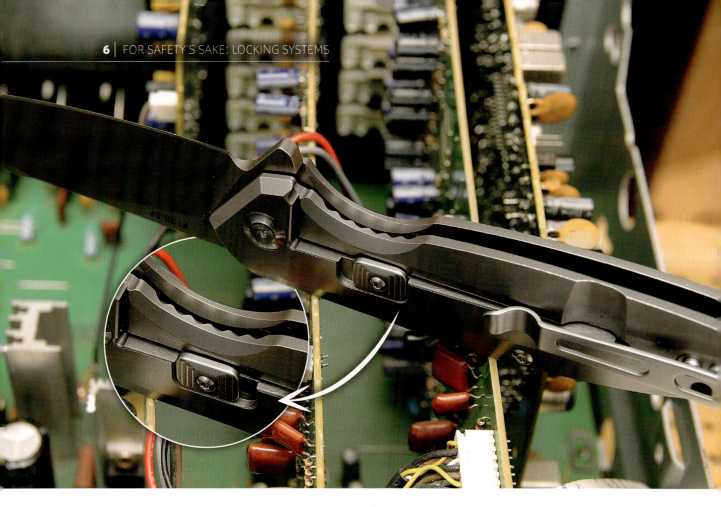

In additional locking systems for frame locks, a slider prevents the spring bar from moving out.

In order to lock the blade securely, for a frame lock it's recommended that the lock bar in new condition should cover at least 25% of the ramp (as seen from above). The same principles as with the liner lock apply regarding the angle. Therefore, it also experiences the same problems if the ramp has not been correctly manufactured. By and large, the frame lock is considered to be less prone to failure than the liner lock.

Manufacturers have also developed additional safety-locking systems, which are included in many models. They generally work according to similar principles as the LAWKS. Via a small slider, a bar is positioned between the overtravel stop and the handle scales, and in this way, the lock bar cannot move away from the ramp. Depending on the manufacturer, there are the most-varied names for these additional locking systems. Also, the arrangement and design of the slider are very different, but the basic principle is more or less the same.

As with a liner lock, the wear and tear that occurs over time is accommodated by the design. Furthermore, modern frame locks are generally also equipped with a separate lock bar insert of steel. As a result, there is barely any wear and tear, but then of course the strong locking friction effect of the titanium is lost. The more recent generations from Chris Reeve have a small ball of extremely hard technical ceramic on the front of the lock bar. This ball touches the tang and at the same time functions as a detent ball. Most manufacturers screw small lock bar insert made of steel to the front of the bar.

They are often designed so that you can move them to adjust the locking system. The screwed-in stoppers have the advantage that if required, they can be replaced. On many of the modern folding knives, they are additionally designed so that they also function as the overtravel stop.

With a frame lock made of titanium, a stopper made of steel prevents wear and tear and usually also serves as an overtravel stop.

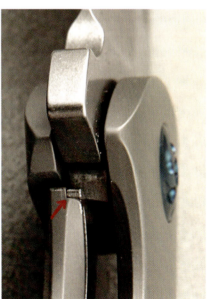

Photo: MM / Oliver Lang

THE IMPULSE BUY

Whereas clipped-on folding knives are usually not even noticed by most people, knife enthusiasts pay them a different kind of attention. A clip is an instant source of curiosity: you wonder what kind of knife is hiding in the trouser pocket. Experienced knife enthusiasts can often recognize the knife manufacturer just by seeing the clip. For me, such clip curiosity led me to an impulse buy. At the Knife Show in Solingen, I saw something on the pocket of knife maker Janusz "Micho" Kozolubski. And what he pulled out triggered a huge "must have" feeling in me.

The knives by Janusz can be bought from Polish Custom Knives (polishcustomknives.com). In addition to his own creations, he also enjoys "pimping" premium series knives and enhancing them in his own special way. That evening, I returned home not just with a lighter wallet but with a real treasure. As experienced knife enthusiasts may recognize, this unique folding knife began life as a Zero Tolerance 0560. The series version of the design by Rick Hinderer is equipped with a titanium frame lock, a 3-D-milled G-10 front scale, ball bearings, and a blade made of Elmax steel. Janusz decorated the blade and the clip with a hand-drilled pattern. The titanium components were heat colored, and the front scale was given a new structure and covered with sturgeon leather, which gives the folding knife a real primitive look. A particular treat was the small skull installed into the end of the handle.

Back locks: Maserin Nimrod · Spyderco Stretch · CRKT Graphite. (The latter image shows the Klecker lock developed by Glenn Klecker. In this variation of the back lock, the scoring is an integral part of the steel frame.)

THE BACK LOCK

The back lock is one of the old tried-and-tested locking systems and can be found on a lot of old-school pocketknives. Even modern outdoor knives tend to favor the back lock, primarily because the back lock has proven itself to be more resistant than liner locks or frame locks against transverse pressure; for example, as occurring during rough carving.

On traditional pocketknives, such as the Buck 110, the lever is positioned on the back end of the handle, whereas it's found in the center of modern practical folding knives, which facilitates one-handed use. This design gained popularity primarily through the original model of the Al Mar *SERE*. To emphasize the difference from traditional back locks, terms such as front lock or midlock were used for these models in the 1980s and 1990s, but they did not become established in the long term. Today, we generally say back lock.

On a back lock, the hook-shaped end of a locking lever is pressed into a matching recess in the tang through spring pressure. At the same time, the locking system functions as a stopper, and there is no designated stop pin. When the knife is closed, the hook presses against the underside of the tang and, as a result, builds resistance against opening. Even if there are

6 | FOR SAFETY'S SAKE: LOCKING SYSTEMS

THE BACK LOCK

This image shows the traditional structure of the back-lock mechanism.

Photo: Fronteddu/Steigerwald

differences in the details (e.g., size of hook and recess, the angle that they are worked into, or how far the hook is inserted into the recess), the fundamental principle is always the same. However, there are very distinct differences in the springs which press into the locking lever, since they can be designed in various ways.*

On some modern back locks, there is a small dent on the locking lever. It's used as a thumb hold and facilitates use. This dent is was invented by American knife maker David Boye and is threfore called the Boye dent. It's used, for example, in nearly all back locks on Spyderco knives.

With a back lock, the mechanical inertia of the closed blade is significantly greater than with a liner lock as a result of the spring pressure. When opening the knife, you have to overcome the resistance, which is noticeably stronger. But you also need more force to unlock it. It can be tricky to close the knife with one hand, because if your thumb is pressing on the locking lever, you cannot use your index finger to fold in the blade. Therefore, you either have to push the knife into its handle from its spine (e.g., by pressing it against

---

* All important details on how they function can be found in the book *The Lockback Folding Knife* by Stefan Steigerwald and Peter Fronteddu.

your leg). Or you have to hold the knife horizontally and gently shake it so that the blade swings down. However, the only way you can do this without risk of injury is when your index finger is protected by a ricasso. Then, it's possible to fold it back into place by pressing the back lock with your thumb.

All in all, it's far more comfortable and a lot easier to use a knife with a liner lock than one with a back lock. However, depending on the design, there are significant differences between back locks. These differences not only are down to the lever configuration but are also caused by the blade position and the sesign of the locking lever. Modern back lock knives with blades on ball bearings and softer spring systems are much easier to open and close.

Over time, there may be wear and tear on the contact point between the tang and the locking hook. Signs of this wear and tear are primarily a slight radial slackness of the blade (in the direction of the turn) and the lever sinking deeper into the handle when the blade is open. Increased wear and tear on the hook may prevent it from being able to correctly lock.

Fluff and dirt from trouser pockets may also accumulate in the tang recess and prevent the hook from going far enough into it. In this case, regular cleaning is required. However, the aforementioned problems only happen occasionally. All in all, the back lock is very safe. However, under extreme (!) stress, the back lock has been known to fail. It's generally the hook piece or its counterpart in the blade tang that breaks. Whether this failure is due to lacking material thickness or, rather, material defects has not yet been sufficiently researched.

THE TRI-AD LOCK

In 2008, the American company Cold Steel presented an improvedversion of the back lock: the Tri-Ad lock, based on a design by American knife maker John PerMar. His patent was bought by Cold Steel, and it was further developed by knife designer Andrew Demko, who worked for Cold Steel for

Placing the back lock in the center of the handle makes it possible to close a knife with one hand. (Spyderco Stretch XL)

6 | FOR SAFETY'S SAKE: LOCKING SYSTEMS

Details of the Tri-Ad lock:
1) additional stop pin
2) slightly angled lock hook
3) extra space, for wear and tear
4) rocker pin with extra space, which compensates for the wear and tear

Nearly all folding knives from Cold Steel, such as the Espada, are equipped with a Tri-Ad lock.

many years. Since then, the majority of foldign knives by Cold Steel have been equipped with a Tri-Ad lock.

In terms of material, the Tri-Ad lock has been made significantly stronger than the majority of back locks. In addition, on the Tri-Ad lock, the lock hook and recess in the contact area have been shaped on a slight angle so that they lock more securely. This area is also designed to have extra space so that wear and tear can be accommodated.

The key difference between back locks and Tri-Ad locks is an additional, strong stop pin, which matches to a recess in the tang. That has several effects: first, on impact there is a better distribution of forces, and second, wear and tear is also accommodated in this way. Pressure on the opened blade (from both the spine and the cutting edge) is directed via the stop pin to the frame, instead of being concentrated on the lock hook.

140

To prove the toughness of the Tri-Ad lock system, Cold Steel hung a whole engine block from it in a series of tests.

Photo: Cold Steel

THE MUDD FOLDING KNIFE

Usually, practical folding knives are designed for general everyday work. But you also come across special designs for particular categories of use. One example is the MUDD folding knife, constructed by knife-making duo Grant and Gavin Hawk. The acronym stands for "multi utility dirt defiant" and at the same time is also a play on the word "mud." Father and son Hawk designed it as a knife for working in extremely dirty and damp conditions. It's a pocketknife that does not suffer from exposure to water, sand, and other elements. To protect it, the MUDD's pivot mechanism, locking system, and their operating elements were given an all-around rubber seal. The MUDD is a design that is as innovative as it's unique. A series version was produced by Zero Tolerance, but sadly, only for a short time.

Photo: Sharp by Coop

In regard to safety, the Tri-Ad lock has proven to be almost unbreakable. Cold Steel likes to demonstrate its prowess on videos with extreme stress tests. The disadvantage is that the Tri-Ad lock is noticeably more difficult to unlock—you need a little trick to do so: when pressing your thumb on the lever, your index finger needs to be placed at the same height on the opposite side of the handle as a support.

With the axis lock, the crossways bar moves along a short runner and is pressed against the tang by the omega spring.

Photo: MM / Oliver Lang

AXIS LOCK & CO.

Several locking mechanisms are based on a short steel bar that sits across the handle. These mechanisms can for the most part be traced back to the axis lock brought onto the market in 1998 by Benchmade. The inventors of the axis lock were knife makers Bill McHenry and Jason Williams. The system was first used in the Benchmade 710, which they designed. The knife was one of Benchmade's bestsellers for nearly twenty years, but it's now no longer produced.

The heart of the system is a round steel bar of approximately 0.12 in. diameter, which sits crossways in the handle. When the knife is opened, the crossways bar is pressed into a recess of the tang by two omega springs.

These springs are shaped like the Greek letter Ω and sit in flat pockets in the handle scales. The crossways bar moves along a short runner, which is carved from the liner on each side. From the outside, you can access the bar through slits in the handle scales. In order to unlock it, it's pulled back away from the tang against the spring pressure.

The axis lock is a very strong and safe locking system that can withstand an awful lot of pressure—either the crossways bar itself or the liner would

The legendary Benchmade 710 was the first knife with an axis lock.

Photo: Benchmade

Photo: Spyderco

OTHER BAR SYSTEMS

Over the course of the years, many mechanisms have come on to the market that, like the axis lock, are based on a crossways bolt with spring pressure, but the details of the systems are different, for example, the Arc Lock from SOG. The crossways bar is not positioned in a straight runner but in a curved one. The system guarantees additional safety when the knife is closed, ensuring that the blade cannot accidentally open out. These days, SOG no longer uses the Arc lock, and their current system, the XR lock, corresponds largely to the axis lock.

Other locking systems are based on similar principles to the axis lock but do not use the omega spring and crossways bars. For example, the ball bearing lock from Spyderco uses an approximately 0.15-in. diameter steel ball that is pressed into a recess in the tang by a coil spring (*photo*). To unlock it, the ball is pulled back against the spring, which is not easy with damp hands, and not always possible with gloves. For this reason, Spyderco has been sandwiching the ball between two sliders for several years now. It allows easier use of the ball bearing lock, but the details of the snazzy mechanism can no longer be seen.

The bolt action lock is similar but has a special role. It's an invention of the late knife maker Walter "Blackie" Collins and is older than the original axis lock. It's a steel bar which does not lie crossways but lengthways in the handle and is moved by a coil spring.

FOR SAFETY'S SAKE: LOCKING SYSTEMS | 6

have to yield for it to fail. The wear and tear regulates itself because the springs simply push the crossways bar a bit farther up the ramp on the tang. Only after years of intensive use would it be possible for the springs to lose some of their tension and need to be replaced.

Alongside its high level of safety, it has the great advantage that the axis lock is very simple and intuitive to use—by both left- and right-handers. Furthermore, when folding the knife, your fingers are not in the way of the blade. From the point of view of many knife enthusiasts, the axis lock represents a very good combination of a high level of safety and a high level of user comfort. The underlying patent protection of the axis lock has now expired, but its name is still legally protected.

Nowadays, there are many manufacturers who have developed their own versions of axis lock systems: for example, the Slide-Lock (Real Steel), Able Lock (Hogue), or A-Lock (Acta Non Verba). The knife community is therefore looking for a collective term for systems that are practically the same as the axis lock. Many knife enthusiasts now use the factually correct term "crossbar lock."

OTHER LOCKING SYSTEMS

Compression Lock

This is a special locking system designed by Spyderco and added to their models that are designed to have a high level of safety. At first glance, it looks like a liner lock turned on its head. However, its mechanisms work differently: the spring locks between the tang and the stop pin, which makes slipping off almost impossible. However, what's more important is that forces vertically exerted on the blade are conducted away into the liner by the stop pin.

The compression lock is more reliable and more robust than the liner

When opening the knife, the bar slips over the curve of the tang and is pressed onto the flat back of the tang from behind by the spring. The crossbar lock is very tough.

Opposite: After the patent expired, an increasing number of companies have started bringing their own version of the axis locks onto the market. (Acta non Verba A200 · Real Stell Huginn · Herbertz Selektion)

145

6 | FOR SAFETY'S SAKE: LOCKING SYSTEMS

On the compression lock, the spring lock is wedged between the stop pin and the tang.

locks and frame locks. In addition, you have the advantage that your fingers are not positioned in front of the blade as it folds in. However, using it is not so simple, and it takes a little more practice. In particular with flipper knives, there's a risk you may jam your fingertips in the engaging compression lock when opening the knife until you become familiar with the system.

Deadbolt lock

The deadbolt lock, developed by knife maker Flavio Ikoma, is a locking system that is used on the CRKT knives. While its operation through pressure on the pivot pin is reminiscent of the legendary Paul Knives, a completely different mechanism is concealed within the system. Its centerpiece is a solid anchor made of steel, which fully protrudes through the liner and the back scale on the right side. When closed, this anchor is pressed outward by the tang.

When the blade is opened the anchor slides inward. In doing so, one arm of the anchor moves through a hole in the right liner and into the tang, while the second arm even reaches farther through the left liner. Therefore, the blade is anchored in three different places at the same time. By placing pressure on the spring-loaded pivot pin cover, the anchor is pressed outward again and the blade can be closed.

The deadbolt is mechanically extremely tough. Either the liner or the tang needs to break for the locking system to fail... and it would be pretty far-fetched for the construction to break in several places at once. In my own practical tests, the deadbolt lock made good on its promises. Cutting through branches was absolutely no

FOR SAFETY'S SAKE: LOCKING SYSTEMS | 6

Photo: CRKT

The deadbolt lock is unlocked by putting pressure on the pivot pin. (CRKT Linchpin)

The deadbolt lock anchors the blade to the liners in three places.

6 | FOR SAFETY'S SAKE: LOCKING SYSTEMS

The centerpiece of the button lock is a spring-loaded steel bolt with a conical head.

problem with this locking system. Even a very rough spine-whacking test left absolutely no impression on the deadbolt lock. Despite brutally hitting the blade spine on a wood board, the locking system did not budge a millimeter.

Apart from its extreme reliability, the deadbolt lock has even more plus points. First, it's very easy and intuitive to use. Thanks to the size of the press button, it can even be unlocked easily when wearing gloves. And very importantly, fingers don't get caught by the closing blade. The only negative of the deadbolt lock is that the anchor piece in the back scale detracts from its appearance.

Button lock

This mechanism is operated via a button on the front scale that is connected to a conical sprung bolt. When not in use, the bolt presses into a lock-in position of the tang. It holds the blade in the handle without locking it. When it's being opened, the bolt is pushed by the tang against the spring pressure a bit farther into the back scale. As soon as the blade is fully opened the spring presses the bolt into a recess in the tang. As a result, the blade is locked.

The head of the bolt slots into a recess in the tang.

To unlock it, you press the bolt back into the back scale, using the external button.

A properly designed button lock is a locking system that is safe and, above all, very comfortable to use. One of its other advantages is that your fingers are not positioned in the blade's trajectory when closing the blade. It's very intuitive and easy to use because the spring pressure is usually not very high.

However, the button lock is relatively sensitive to fibers and fluff. If the knife is carried in trouser pockets for a long time without being used, and fibers collect in the recess in the tang, it's possible that the bolt will not go far enough in, and as a result the blade will not lock properly. Therefore, button lock knives should be regularly maintained and cleaned.

A further problem is a badly designed button lock. For example, if it doesn't go deep enough into the recess in the tang, so that any unintentional slight pressure on the button could lead to it unlocking. For heavy cutting work, Hogue has furnished its designs with additional safety-locking systems, which prevent the button lock from accidentally being unlocked.

Three knives with button locks. (Hogue EX-03 · Spartan Pallas · Civivi Cogent)

6 | FOR SAFETY'S SAKE: LOCKING SYSTEMS

Different locking systems: Bolster lock (Liong Mah Get Shit Done), axis lock (Benchmade 710), frame lock (Defcon Mako), button lock (Real Steel Griffin), Compression lock (Spyderco Amalgam) and Klecker Lock (CRKT Tighe Rod)

FOR SAFETY'S SAKE: LOCKING SYSTEMS | **6**

CHAPTER 7
WITH ONE HAND: OPENING MECHANISMS

The ability to use a knife with one hand is an essential element of a practical folding knife. Above all, it's essential for rescuers and law enforcement officers: "I can only emphasize again and again that in many situations it's essential to be able to use the knife with one hand," explains Jürgen Sohnemann, the former German SWAT officer and police expert who developed the Spyderco Ulize together with knife maker Uli Hennicke. But civilian users have also recognized the advantages of one-handed operation for their work, leisure time, and everyday life.

One-handed knives are much more comfortable to use than old-school pocketknives—that alone is already sufficient enough reason to prefer them. Furthermore, they are also safer: a common cause of cuts is when you need to keep ahold of whatever you are cutting and it's impossible to safely close the traditional pocketknife, so that you put it down with the blade open. As soon as you need the knife again, you reach for it—and unfortunately grab the sharp

"The readiness is all."

–William Shakespeare -

blade. That doesn't happen with a one-handed knife because you can close it without letting go of what you are cutting.

One-handed use doesn't just mean opening the knife with one hand, but also closing it with one hand. And as we saw in the last chapter, some systems (e.g., liner, frame, button, or axis locks) are much better suited to both one-handed opening and closing than other systems (e.g., the back lock). The comfortable, swift, and smooth one-handed use of a pocketknife depends on four interconnected factors:

- locking system
- blade bearing
- proper adjusted blade motion
- design of the blade lifter

Opposite: **In recent years, the flipper has become the most popular opening mechanism.**

7 | WITH ONE HAND: OPENING MECHANISMS

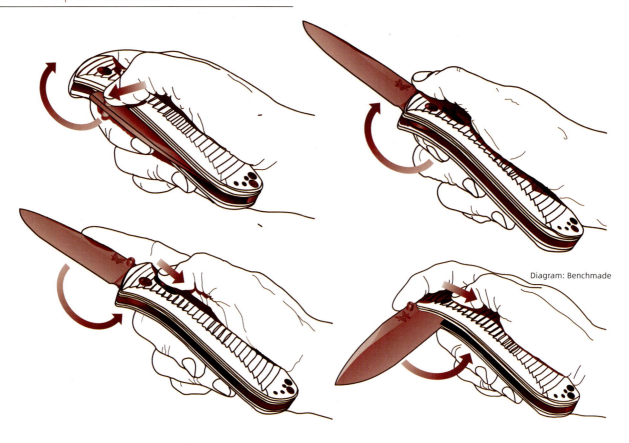

Diagram: Benchmade

One-handed use doesn't just mean opening the knife with one hand, but also closing it with one hand, shown here using the axis lock as an example.

BLADE BEARINGS

Whether the blade has a correct motion depends very much on the blade bearing (e.g., Does the blade move smoothly in its intended path between the handle scales?). It's therefore a question of keeping the friction as low as possible. There are two types of blade bearings: sliding washers and ball bearings.

Washers should have the largest possible diameter. The larger the diameter, the better the pressure is distributed, the more smoothly the blade moves, and the better the blade motion can be adjusted. Washers can be made of various materials. For affordable knives, they are often made of plastic. In many models, they are made of Teflon, which is used in frying pans for its antistick properties. Teflon repels dirt and therefore is low maintenance. However, Teflon is not very resistant to pressure, which is noticeable particularly in thinner sliding washers. The blade is not very laterally stable, meaning you need to screw the pivot pin tighter—which makes the blade motion.

For high-quality knives, the washers are made of bronze (to be more exact, phosphor bronze). Bronze is significantly more pressure resistant and dimensionally stable that Teflon; however, small particles of dust are not repelled. Therefore, bronze is more

154

WITH ONE HAND: OPENING MECHANISMS

Photo: MM/Oliver Lang

likely to become dirty and requires more maintenance. Yet, bronze washers have the great advantage that they allow less sideways slackness of the blade. The blade motion can be more precisely adjusted and doesn't need to be re-adjusted as often.

Ever more frequently, you find ball bearings instead of sliding washers on modern pocketknives. They significantly reduce the friction, they let the blade move more smoothly, and they also require less maintenance. While sliding washers made of Teflon or bronze need regular lubrication, it's not required as often for ball bearings. As a rule, real maintenance is only needed if the mechanism gets dirty.

There are a few variations of ball bearing washers for knife blades. One of the most widespread is the IKBS (Ikoma Korth Ball Bearing System), developed by Brazilian knife makers Flavio Ikoma and Rick Lala (Korth Knives). Today, high-quality knives normally use ball bearings made of technical ceramic.

There are also critical opinions about ball bearings among knife enthusiasts. Some people think that they are less tough than bronze washers in regard to the sideways slackness. However, the sideways slackness has less to do with the ball bearings themselves and is more about the construction of the tang and the handle scales, and

Teflon washer in the SR1 Lite by Cold Steel. The details of the Tri-Ad-Lock can be clearly seen.

7 | WITH ONE HAND: OPENING MECHANISMS

BALL BEARINGS

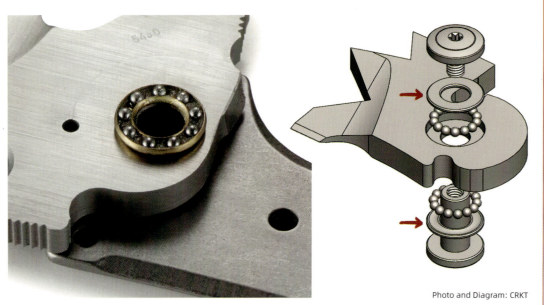

Ball bearings for pocketknives can be designed in different ways. In the IKBS system by Flavio Ikoma and Rick Lala, it also includes additional washers.

Photo and Diagram: CRKT

Opposite: **The CRKT Fossil was one of the first pocketknives that used the IKBS ball bearing system.**

their interplay with the ball bearings (i.e., whether the recess is correctly designed and if the ball bearing really fits into it). Incidentally, that goes for normal washers as well. If they have a poor design or are poorly manufactured (or both), it can result in sideways slackness and problems with the blade motion. In addition, you also need to be mindful of correct usage: EDC flippers with ball bearings are simply not designed as crowbars for use with high transverse pressure.

A further argument against ball bearing washers is the wear and tear: with constant use, they will burnish grooves into the tang, resulting in a sideways slackness that can no longer be fixed. In fact, when frequently used flippers are taken apart, you often see clear grooves that the ball bearings, primarily ceramic ball bearing washers, have left in the liners, which are typically made of relatively soft steel or titanium. Such grooves are created by extensive "constant flipping," but as a rule, they are generally not so deep for practical problems to occur; for instance, blade slackness that can no longer be fixed. In the few observed cases, the cause is much more likely a material defect than the ball bearings

WITH ONE HAND: OPENING MECHANISMS | 7

7 | WITH ONE HAND: OPENING

Photo: Pohl Force

Proper adjustment of blade motion is very important. Here, designer Dietmar Pohl is lending a hand at the Lion Steel workshop.

To avoid sideways slackness, it's important that the ball bearings are fitted well.

Photo: MM /Oliver Lang

A blade positioned in the exact center of the handle when closed indicates high-quality manufacturing.

themselves. In high-quality knives, there are usually additional washers between the ball bearings and the liner, and these washers can be replaced in the case of any burnishing.

BLADE MOTION

With liner lock and frame lock models in particular, but also with other designs, it frequently happens that the blade motion changes when the knife is regularly used or was incorrectly adjusted at the factory. Typical examples are:

• The blade is not positioned centrally in the handle but is pressed into the opposite liner and scrapes along it when opening and closing the knife.

• The blade sticks, does not open smoothly, and can be opened only slowly or with a lot of force.
• The blade develops a sideward slackness, and there are problems with the locking system.

In such cases, you can adjust the blade motion by loosening or tightening the pivot pin. However, that must be done within a certain tolerance so that the knife still works properly. Ball bearings allow for a significantly larger tolerance range than Teflon or bronze washers, and the pivot pin can be screwed tighter. If the problems are not solved by adjusting the pivot pin, it sometimes helps to swap the washers from one side to another, provided they have the same diameter.

7 | WITH ONE HAND: OPENING MECHANISMS

EMERSON WAVE

The Wave is a special blade lifter invented by Ernest Emerson. As the founder of Emerson Knives, he also shaped a wavelike hook on the far end of the blade spine in addition to the thumb disk. When drawing the knife from your pocket, if you pull it back, the wave-shaped hook latches onto the edge of the pocket. As a result of the pulling movement, the blade is instantly opened. However, the wave has one disadvantage: regular usage leads to considerable wear and tear on the trousers because it causes the pocket seam to fray.

7 WITH ONE HAND: OPENING MECHANISMS

LIFTER ACTION

So that a blade lifter functions properly, it needs to have enough distance and height offset to the pivot pin.

Photo: CRKT

If the blade does not move smoothly, you should try applying a little oil before adjusting the pivot pin. Under no circumstance should you use any old oil from the hardware store. Larger knife merchants have high-quality special oil in their range for this purpose. As a rule, the oil dispensers are also equipped with thin tubes that enable you to reach the pivot pin without having to completely dismantle the knife or drown it in oil. Alternatively, you can apply the oil as a fine spray and, in doing so, dose it precisely.

Many pivot nuts have a flat section on one side that prevent them from turning with the screw. If the nut turns as well, a good tip is to press a rubber against the head from the opposite side. As a rule, it creates enough adhesion to be able to turn the screw on its own.

BLADE LIFTERS

The thumb-operated blade lifters come in a variety of basic shapes. However, for comfortable one-handed use, it's not just the shape that is decisive but also the complete design of the blade-lifting system. That means that irrespective of its shape, a blade lifter must also

- deploy adequate leverage
- and be easily accessible for thumbs.

The longer the lever, the less force is required. This law of physics also applies to one-handed knives and in our case

161

7 | WITH ONE HAND: OPENING MECHANISMS

Folding knives with thumb pins: United Cutlery Wolfhound · Benchmade Snody Gravitator · CRKT My Tighe · Real Steel S6

means that the bigger the distance between the blade lifter and the blade pivot, the smaller the force required. However, as a result, the distance that the thumb needs to travel increases. In practice, the height offset to the blade pivot is also important. These dimensions are limited by the knife width and thumb length.

It's easy to see if the distance is too short, since it makes the blade lifter difficult to use. This is particularly the case with very slim and delicate knives. Slim knives are best opened with a flipper because the leverage is then created in another way.

To be used easily, the blade lifter on the closed knife needs to be easily accessible to the thumb.

To solve this problem, cutouts and flat sections are worked into the handle to make the blade lifter more accessible and also guide the thumb toward it.

There are three basic types of blade lifters that are operated by the thumb:

- thumb pin
- thumb disk
- thumbhole

The thumb pin is the most-used type. It's usually mounted on both sides so

WITH ONE HAND: OPENING MECHANISMS | 7

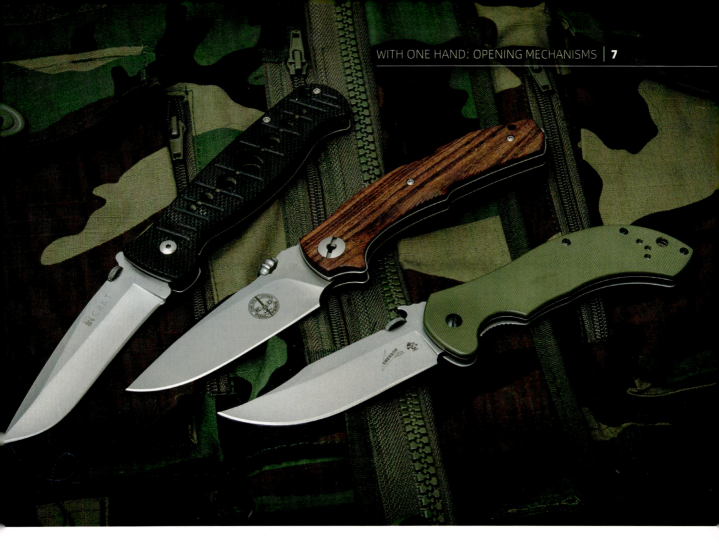

that left-handers can also use it. Fortunately, one-sided thumb pins are only rare these days. On cheaper models, the thumb pin is often only glued in place, but on better-quality knives it's screwed on.

Bob Tezuola's ATCF and many other knives are not equipped with thumb pins but with thumb disks. This disk is mounted horizontally on the blade spine. Modern series-made knives (e.g., the knives from Emerson) are generally equipped with a thumb disk. In contrast to the thumb pin, the disk has the advantage that it's significantly easier to use in gloves. For that reason, the trusty PRT (Pocket Rescue Tool) rescue knives by Eickhorn are equipped with a large thumb disk. Thumb discs generally come in the same shape (a round disk with a knurled edge), but there are also designer pieces in fancy shapes.

The thumbhole goes back to Spyderco and the first modern one-handed knife. Spyderco founder Sal Glesser was seeking an alternative to the thumb pin for one-handed use. In his opinion, the pin would not only catch on trouser pockets when drawing it, but it was also in the way when cutting. However, that would only be the case

Folding knives with thumb disks: CRKT Falcon · Pohl Force Mike Five · Kershaw CQC-10K

7 | WITH ONE HAND: OPENING MECHANISMS

A large thumbhole is extremely functional; however, it also greatly affects the appearance.

if you were cutting something with a large surface area (e.g., cutting off a slice of bread). In any case, Sal was tinkering with another solution in 1980. His idea was not to screw something on, but to take something away. After several attempts to put recesses on both sides of the blade, he eventually had a complete break-through and the result was the large, round thumbhole. While other brands feature thumbholes in various other shapes, Spyderco has legally protected the circular thumbhole. It became a trademark of the manufacturer. Even on the fixed-blade Spyderco knives, there is also a small, round hole in the blade, even though it has no function at all.

In terms of functionality, the thumbhole is a solution that's as simple as it's practical. However, in terms of appearance, many knife enthusiasts are not so keen because the thumbhole influences the look of the knife more than any other kind of blade lifter. It often becomes the dominant element

Photo: Spyderco

of the knife and frequently leads to the Spyderco-typical leaf-shaped and almost triangular blade profile, or to marked bulges. Only in rare cases has a large thumbhole design been incorporated in the whole general look of a knife.

Different thumbholes: Real Steel Havran · Buck Marksman · Böker Plus Masada · CRKT Fossil

7 | WITH ONE HAND: OPENING MECHANISMS

When open, the flipper lifter often also serves as a hand protector; when closed, it protrudes slightly from the handle's back. (WE Knife 601)

THE FLIPPER

The flipper is currently the most popular opening mechanism for one-handed knives. Blades with ball bearing washers have helped it to an unforeseen success. Until the introduction of the ball bearings, normal blade lifters and flipper knives were more or less equally prevalent. Today, the majority of pocketknives coming onto the market each year are flipper designs.

The flipper is an extension of the tang and protrudes as a small lever on the back of the handle. Flipper is not only used as a name for the mechanism but also as a generic name for this type of knife. The protruding flipper lever is sometimes described more precisely as the flipper tab, but it's generally just known as a flipper.

The flipper works through a lever action. You pull the protruding tab, and the blade pivots on the axis and out of the handle. For simple washers, sometimes an additional movement of the wrist is necessary, but for knives with ball bearing washers a brief pull on the tab is enough. This manner of use is not only very simple but is also a lot of fun, especially when ball bearing systems are involved. Flippers are the one-handed knives that have the biggest fun factor—and for that reason alone they are especially popular.

WITH ONE HAND: OPENING MECHANISMS | 7

For blades with ball bearing washers, a gentle pull of the flipper tab is enough for the blade to swing out.

THUMB PIN VS. FLIPPER

Things that make no difference in everyday life and leisure can be very different in emergency situations: many professional users prefer the traditional thumb blade lifter over the flipper. That's because the different opening mechanisms mean that the knife position will be more or less secure in the hand.

To be able to use the flipper, you sacrifice the most secure hand position: The index finger, which normally forms an ergonomic counterbalance for the thumb, is not there because it's operating the flipper. In emergency situations that could be fatal. You can try this out yourself on knives that have both a traditional blade lifter as well as a flipper.

If you want to know more, American knife expert Michael Janich has carried out a comprehensive analysis of the various opening mechanisms from a tactical point of view. It's available on DVD and as a stream: *Martial Blade Concepts Vol. 6: A Complete Guide to Carrying and Drawing Tactical Folding Knives* (www.martialbladeconcepts.com).

7 | WITH ONE HAND: OPENING MECHANISMS

The flipper tab can take many shapes, although it's often slightly serrated so that the index finger can get a better hold. When the knife is open, the flipper lever also functions as protection for the index finger so that it does not slip onto the blade while working. The flipper tab may be various lengths: shape and size not only affect the appearance, but also how well the knife can be carried and drawn.

Poorly shaped flipper tabs can get caught on the material in your trouser pockets. For blades with good washers and that are properly adjusted, a relatively small flipper tab is enough.

To avoid a flipper tab that disturbs in the pocket, knife makers and the knife industry have come up with several solutions. First, there's the front flipper. It's also an extension of the tang, but it protrudes from the front end of the handle. Depending on the design, the front flipper is used just like a normal flipper with the index finger or thumb. Front flippers have a great advantage in that when the knife is closed, the front flipper aligns with the centerline of the handle, meaning that they aren't problematic in trouser pockets and don't catch. When opened, they disappear between the handle scales. However, front flippers are generally not as comfortable to use as other blade lifters or normal flippers, which means they still only occupy a very niche segment of the market.

The second, even rarer solution is the recessed flipper. This type of construction was made famous primarily by knife maker Keith Ouye. In this design, the flipper tab sits in a recess in the front

Opposite: Flipper tabs can have different shapes and different placements. (Böker Plus Masada · Zero Tolerance 0920 · Real Steel Sea Eagle · Kershaw Junkyard Dog · Civivy Synergy3 · Kizer Begleiter XL)

For a better grip, the flipper lever often has antislip jimpings.

Recessed flippers barely protrude from the spine. (Böker Plus Aluma · Liong Mah Get Shit Done)

Here the thumb disk is also designed as a thumb rest.

Different designs of front flippers

area of the handle instead of protruding from the spine. In this way, it can't get caught in trouser pockets or be otherwise problematic. The recessed flipper works excellently and is just as much fun to use as the normal flipper. It's astonishing why this technically good principle has so far been used so rarely.

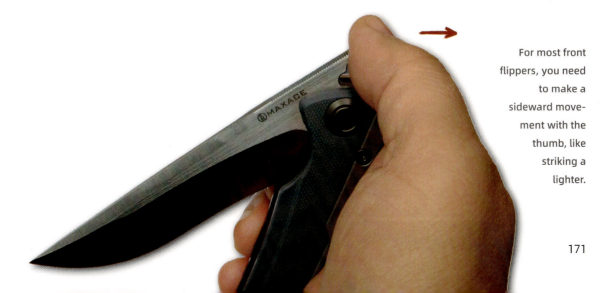

For most front flippers, you need to make a sideward movement with the thumb, like striking a lighter.

7 | WITH ONE HAND: OPENING MECHANISMS

Photos: Böker

Modern tactical switchblades with locking systems: Böker Plus Strike · Böker Plus Intention II

SWITCHBLADE LAWS IN GERMANY

Due to recent restrictions from November 2024, in Germany all switchblades are generally banned. Exceptions are only possible for strong legal reason accompanied with special construction of the switchblade. Legal reasons are occupational use, some sports and if you are an handicapped person, e.g. only have one functional hand.

To plead to these legal reasons, an automatic knife must open to the side (no OTF - Out of The Front), the blade may not be sharpenend on both sides and be less than 3.35 inch in length. All three characteristics have to apply together.

Assisted openers are not legally classed as switchblades. Furthermore, there is also the assessment by the German Federal Police Office (Bundeskriminalamt) (file no. KT21/ZV 25–5164.01-Z-17). Switchblades have blades that "swing out when a button or lever is pressed, and as a result are locked in place." Assisted openers are different because "there is no button or lever to unlock a locking mechanism," as the BKA emphasizes. "This classification also applies for other knives with the above-described manner of function."

However, there are also spring-supported flippers, which according to the BKA are indeed switchblades. And admittedly that is the case, if after pushing the flipper, "the blade fully opens and that happened exclusively thanks to the pressure on the pressurized spring" (file no. SO23–5164.01-Z-389).

WITH ONE HAND: OPENING MECHANISMS | 7

In modern switchblades, the spring is rolled around the pivot. Its angled end fits into a matching recess in the tang.

SWITCHBLADES AND ASSISTED OPENERS

If you look at the range of practical folding knives, automatic knives are but a footnote. It's because nowadays, other designs allow one-handed operation that is just as good, and in many countries, switchblades are either restricted or even completely prohibited by law. In Germany, knife laws concerning swichblades have recently been restricted (see opposite page).

Irrespective of the legal situation, switchblades have been left behind by technical developments. Modern practical folding knives can be easily used with one hand, and compared to switchblades they require less maintenance and are also less likely to succumb to functional defects. After all, switchblades are not exempt from this maxim: The more parts and the more complicated the mechanism, the more venerable the device is. And so even expensive automatic knives experience functional defects. Nowadays, switchblades are valued less for their functionality and more for their technical sophistication.

One-handed knives with spring assistance are relatively common. On an assisted opener, a flipper or blade lifter is used to open the blade up to 30° of the handle, then the spring starts to assist the opening and pushes the blade the remaining way out. By now, nearly all renowned manufacturers also include assisted openers in their

7 | WITH ONE HAND: OPENING MECHANISMS

On an assisted opener, the blade has to be pulled one-third of the way out before the spring begins to work.

As soon as the highest point in the guide channel has been reached, the spring can pull the arm backward.

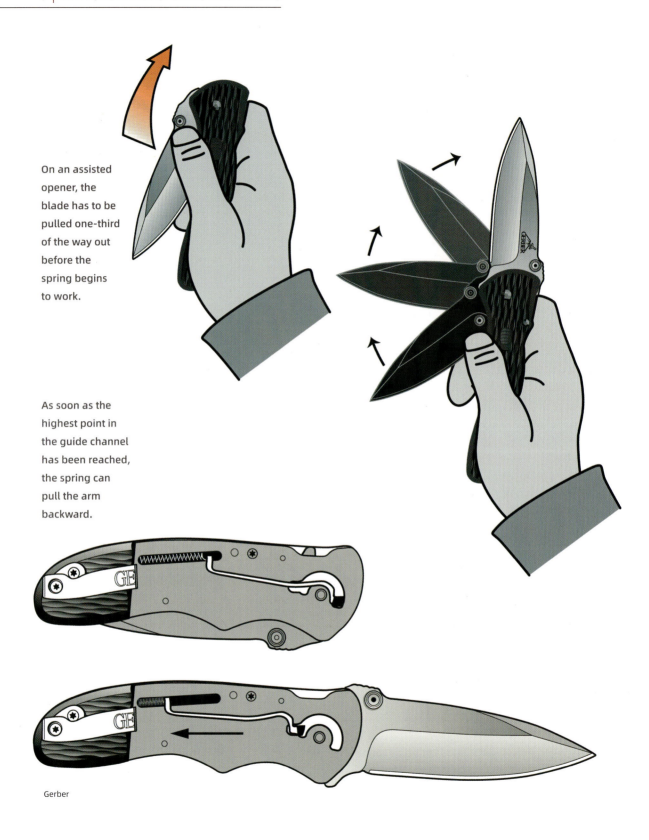

Gerber

WITH ONE HAND: OPENING MECHANISMS

Photos: MM/Wolfgang Peter-Michel

range. The pioneering work was done by Kershaw's Speedsafe model, designed by Ken Onion. In terms of function, assisted openers have no particular advantage over a normal one-handed knife. Above all, manual models with ball bearings can be opened just as comfortably and easily as knives with spring assistance.

In Germany, assisted openers are not classed as switchblades on principle by law. However, there are some assisted openers with flippers that the German Federal Police Office has categorized as prohibited automatic knives (page 172). This legal limbo paints a problematic picture. There are many knife enthusiasts who just can't get on board with an assisted opener. First, they distrust the functioning of the spring. German knife fans additionally fear the legal limbo. However, for these problems there is a relatively simple solution: you can just take out the spring, and as a result an assisted opener is converted into a normal one-handed knife. The mechanisms from the different manufacturers are very different, and so sometimes taking the spring out is very easy and sometimes it's somewhat more complicated.

The spring is usually positioned between the liner and handle scales and can also be removed.

Diagram: Kershaw

The famous Speed Safe System by Ken Onion set a benchmark.

175

7 | WITH ONE HAND: OPENING MECHANISMS

Different opening systems: thumbhole (Spyderco Draper) · thumb pin (SIGtac Pterpdactyl) · flipper (Bestech Starfighter) · front flipper and thumbhole (Bestech Nyxie) · thumb disk and wave (Zero Tolerance 0630)

Photo: CRKT

CHAPTER 8

ALWAYS WITH YOU: THE CLIP

Even if Jethro Gibbs and his rules are just inventions of the *NCIS* TV show scriptwriters, no real-life professional would object to the assertion of rule no. 9. "You should always have a folding knife with you," the former CIA operative Jason Hanson emphasizes in his book, *Spy Secrets That Can Save Your Life*. "It's vital for survival, although you hopefully only have to use it to open cartons or packets of sausages."

The pocketknife is a tool that you should always have on you. For that reason, the clip is the most undervalued detail on modern practical folding knives because it revolutionized how pocketknives are carried.

If you look at all new releases that appear on the knife market each year, it becomes clear that today most pocketknives are equipped with a clip. Even many old-school knives, such as the Buck 110 or Mercator, are now also available as models with a clip. The world of knives can no longer be imagined without pocket clips. The reason for that is very easy: the clip is

"Never go anywhere without a knife."

—Gibbs's Rule no. 9 (NCIS)—

the most practical, the most sensible, and, at the same time, the easiest-to-achieve detail of a modern pocketknife.

Until 1981, there were essentially only two methods of carrying a pocketknife. Large and heavy work knives were carried in a case on the belt, which is not necessarily conducive to everyday life. Or a pocketknife was quite simply put in the trouser pocket, which has several disadvantages. Either the knife instantly falls to the bottom of the pocket, so you have to constantly root through your pockets to find it. Not to mention the fact that a large knife is also uncomfortably noticeable in the pocket. The knife stands outout and, over time, wears through the material of the pocket. In the worst-case scenario, it makes a hole in the

Opposite: **Thanks to the clip, a pocket-knife can be safely and comfortably carried.**

Photo: Spyderco

Spyderco boss Sal Glesser invented the pocketknife clip, which is why the "Spydies" long went by the name Clip-It.

pocket that the knife falls through and gets lost. As someone who in his youth always had a Swiss Army Knife in his pocket, I am speaking from experience—and can tell many tales of woe about regularly finding holes in my pockets.

The solution to all these problems is the pocket clip, which was invented by Spyderco boss Sal Glesser. He got the idea from a clever key chain, which could be hooked onto the edge of trouser pockets. It stopped the keys from falling to the bottom of a pocket and could be used to pull the keys out of the pocket without having to rummage. "I finally put two and two together and decided to mount a clip on the side of the knife, in order for the knife to be close at hand," Sal Glesser explained.

For large pocketknives, the clip has even more advantages: when clipped to the front part of the trouser pocket, the knife sits sideways on the leg, meaning that it moves with the leg when walking. In contrast, a knife that simply lies in the trouser pocket is a dead weight. Furthermore, a pocketknife lying loose in a pocket bulges out much more in the material and is clearly visible. A knife that is clipped in place is much less noticeable.

Even though the clip offers many advantages, there are still some knife users who can't get away with it. Some of them feel that the clip is troublesome in the hand when working. But that has less to do with the clip per se, and more to do with its individual shape and interaction with the handle shape. Another point of criticism is that if you frequently draw and put back the knife, over time it frays the seam of the pocket. That also depends greatly on the clip design and the texture of the handle scales. These days, real "pocket eaters" are only really found among the ranks of military tactical knives. Compared to the damage to the pocket material caused by a loose knife, the slow fraying of the pocket seam is barely worth mentioning.

If you balance these two small criticisms against the great benefits of a clip, it's clear: the clip makes carrying a pocketknife much easier! It even allows large knives to be carried much more comfortably. And the most important thing is that it increases the probability of carrying a knife in the first place. The danger of leaving a knife at home for convenience and then not having it when you need it has been reduced to a minimum.

Unlike his thumbhole, Sal Glesser could not legally protect the clip on the knife—to the sorrow of Spyderco, but to the great happiness of all knife enthusiasts! Yet, in the first years, it was primarily Spyderco models that were equipped with the clip, those "strange pocketknives with the large

THE DISCREET "GIANT KNIFE"

A large pocketknife can draw critical looks. I can well remember a situation when I shared an apartment in my student days: over breakfast, I took a folding knife with a 9.7cm (3.87-in.) blade from my pocket to cut bread, when one of my roommates shouted, "Look what a large knife Thomas has on him!" However, such situations only occur when you open a knife to use it. While it was discreetly clipped into my pocket, none of my roommates noticed at all that I was carrying a knife. By the way, it was the large model of the CRKT Crawford Falcon, which is, sadly, no longer produced. Experience shows that thanks to the clip, large pocketknives can be carried very discreetly. Most people do not notice them—as a rule they are only noticed by trained eyes or other knife enthusiasts.

Photo: CRKT

An extremely rare solution is a spring-loaded clip mounted on the back of the handle.

hole in the blade," as they were seen back then by many buyers. To emphasize the difference to its competitors, in the first twenty years, the pocketknives from Spyderco were generally given the affix "Clip-It" to their names in order to draw attention to this special feature.

In the early 1990s, the idea of the clip began to spread rampantly. The great success of Bob Terzuola's ATCF was also a contributing factor. For the first time ever, he attached a pocket clip to a handmade custom knife. Already by the mid-1990s, most companies that made modern knives were mounting pocket clips. Nowadays, you see them on almost every practical folding knife.

LEFT OR RIGHT, TIP DOWN OR TIP UP?

According to statistics, 85% to 90% of everyone in the world is right-handed. And accordingly, most practical folding knives are designed for right-handers. In addition to the ramifications for the design of the locking system, it also means that the clip is primarily attached to the right side of the knife. Of course, a left-hander can also clip such a knife to their left trouser pocket, but it would be the wrong way round so that after pulling out the knife, they would have to turn it in their hand before being able to open it and use it. And with it, a lot of the handling comfort is lost. To accommodate the left-handed

ACTIONABLE CLIPS

To accommodate left-handed knife enthusiasts, some models offer the option of moving the clip to the other side.

Whether you carry your knife tip down or tip up is above all a matter of personal taste. There are also models where you can convert the pocket clip to suit either method of carrying.

Diagrams: Kershaw

On the topic of deep pocket carry, there are some very different solutions (e.g., standard tip up, deep carry, and the movable Mobilip clip).

customer group, many practical folding knives also offer the option of moving the clip from the right to the left side.

Another point is the question of whether a clip should be mounted for carrying tip down or tip up. As a rule, tip down has the disadvantage that after drawing the knife, you need to reposition it in your hand so that you are ready to work. However, if the clip is attached for tip up, then the knife is ready for work immediately after being pulled out of the pocket. A further point is that a tip-down mounted clip is generally more uncomfortable in the hand than a tip-up mounted clip.

In the 1980s and 1990s, clips were generally mounted for tip-down carrying, since that was considered safer. For liner lock models with a less defined detent ball, there was the danger that if carried tip up in the pocket, it would partially open. When reaching for the knife, you might grab the blade.

With increasingly better-designed liner locks, this danger has now been reduced to a minimum. Today the majority of clips are mounted for tip-up carrying.

Some practical folding knives offer the option of attaching the clip either for tip-up or tip-down carrying. Spyderco even provides for many knives the option of attaching the clip in four different positions: right, left, tip up, and tip down. However, the disadvantage of the convertible clip is that for every carrying option, corresponding holes must be drilled into the handle scales, which does not really look pretty. Furthermore, as a rule they require standard clips—milled designs can normally only be mounted in one position.

DEEP CARRY AND REAR MOUNTING

There are two different philosophies concerning carrying a practical folding knife. One says that the knife should be carried so it can be drawn as quickly and easily as possible; therefore, the clip is mounted so that a small piece of the handle protrudes from the pocket. The other philosophy emphasizes that the knife should disappear as far as possible into the pocket, so that it's not noticeable. That is not only important for professional users and those deployed undercover, but also for civilian knife enthusiasts, who live and work in an environment where carrying a knife may cause offense and unpleasant discussions. For that reason, many modern folding knives have a deep-carry clip.

This deep-carry clip is designed so that it forms a loop-shaped arc above

MODERNIZED CLASSIC KNIVES

Army pocketknives go back to the nineteenth century. Alongside trench daggers and other combat knives, a practical cutting tool has been needed in military missions since time immemorial. One of the most popular models was the Mercator knife from Solingen. The simple pocketknife with the handle made of grooved sheet steel and a back lock was developed back in 1867. Although it was not an official piece of equipment, it was popular among German soldiers in the First World War.

Recently, modernized models of the Mercator have been made (e.g., with stainless steel, handles made of brass, and, last but not least, with the pocket clip). The Mercator Clip is a beautiful and very functional version of a classic pocketknife.

Photo: Otter

There are very different, more or less elegant, solutions for mounting a clip on the back of a knife.

the screw holes. This loop is almost flush with the back end of the knife, so that only the clip can actually be seen in the pocket. For a knife to be less noticeable depends not only on how deep it disappears into the pocket, but also on the size, shape, and color of the clip.

A technically unique deep-carry clip is the Mobilip clip from Tekut. The clip is mounted to be movable: as soon as the knife goes into the pocket, the clip pushes itself a little out of the handles, so that the knife goes farther inside the pocket and can be carried without attracting attention. That makes sense, but the Mobilip clip does require some practice to pull it in and out of your pocket smoothly.

Deep-carry clips for back mounting are an elegant and practical solution. They are not screwed to the side of the handle scales, but right at the back on the backspacer. It has two advantages: first, the clip can be very elegantly and simply turned from right to left, and second, ugly drilled holes in the handle scales are not necessary.

TYPES OF CLIPS

According to the method of production, there are three different types of clips:

- die-cut clips
- wire clips
- milled clips

The die-cut clips form the biggest group by far. They are die-cut from sheet steel and bent into shape. Die-

cut clips are generally screwed onto the liners through the handle scales, and often also to the backspacer, and held in place with two or three small Torx head screws. You can find these clips in all kinds of shapes and sizes. Generally, they are symmetrical, but you sometimes also find asymmetrical ones or models with a slight arch tailored to the curved handle. However, asymmetrical clips cannot be attached to the other side of the handle, so that the manufacturers have to include a second, mirror-inverted clip. Large and well-known manufacturers such as Spyderco and Benchmade use standardized clip shapes that fit the majority of models in their range.

Wire clips are made of strong spring wire. Because wire clips are less noticeable than die-cut clips, they are a particularly discreet and elegant solution. The disadvantage is that, to affix the wire clip, two small slits in the handle scale are needed and a significantly larger screw is required.

Clips milled from solid materials are generally used on expensive knives. They are made mainly of titanium and occasionally from carbon. As a rule, milled clips are tailored to the design of the handle and often have the same color as the handle. Compared to steel clips, clips made of titanium are significantly less elastic. Therefore, these clips often have a small swell on the end that holds the knife in position in the trouser material. On high-quality knives, you find integrated retention balls made out of materials, such as zirconium or ceramic.

From left to right: Die-cut standard clip, wire clip, and 3-D-milled clips made of titanium

Different designs on milled clips: movable roller, shaped, and polished zirconium ball

A lot of things are to be considered when designing a clip. If, for example, the clip on the front end is too pointy, then you can't properly draw the knife. If the clip is sitting tight, you have to use your index finger to push it upward out of your pocket, and that's difficult if a pointed clip's end painfully pierces your fingertip. Other problems include the end of the clip pointing too far inward, so that you can't really get hold of it to pull it out; yet, at the same time, if it sticks too far out, it digs into your palm when you're working.

Furthermore, if it protrudes too far out, it could get caught on something (e.g., in pull cords on fleece jackets or in basket-weave chairs). In the worst-case scenario, the knife is pulled out of your pocket without you noticing and it gets lost.

Compared to milled clips, die-cut clips and wire clips have one big advantage: if the clip is too loose or tight, you can use pliers to correct the tension to some extent. Still, you have to be very careful: too much pressure and the material yields. Less is more is a good maxim in this regard.

No matter what method is used to make it, the clip must fulfill four tasks:

- It must hold the knife securely in position.
- It must allow the knife to be easily and simply drawn and put away.

A CARABINER INSTEAD OF A CLIP

With practical folding knives that are intended for professional use by emergency workers or for specialist sports such as hiking, climbing, or sailing, you often find a carabiner instead of a clip (or in addition to one). There are several reasons for this. First, uniforms or climbing trousers often don't have conventional pockets. Second, it's sometimes also more sensible to attach the knife to the outside of a rucksack rather than to clothing. Furthermore, the knife should also always be accessible when wearing gloves and thick all-weather clothing. And finally, a carabiner is considered to be safer in regard to potentially losing a knife. However, the carabiner hook is just a marginal phenomenon. Although this way of carrying a knife is certainly practical, and you can attach a carabiner hook to the belt loops on any trousers, it has not gained a foothold among EDC pocketknives for daily use.

Photo: Leatherman

The Leatherman Crater has a foldout carabiner hook.

8 | ALWAYS WITH YOU: THE CLIP

Photo: CRKT

It's crucial for all clip designs that the knife can be easily drawn and be securely held in the hand.

- It may not catch on other clothing.
- It should be noticed as little as possible in the hand when working.

Whether these requirements are fulfilled depends on the shape and tension of the clip. Something that may sound trivial is, in practice, a real science.

SPECIAL DESIGNS

So that the clip is not disturbing in the hand, some manufacturers have come up with special solutions for their milled clips. For example, there's the HWAY system by Lion Steel. The "Hide What Annoys You" system works with a retractable clip, which is pulled in using spring pressure and then lies flush with the handle scales. To clip in place, press the button on the other side of the handle to move the clip out of the handle scales.

A retractable clip is very costly to manufacture, which is clearly reflected in the price of the knife. And second, the knife is furnished with a complicated mechanism, which in the long term requires maintenance and care. The recessed clip, which WE Knife presented on its 910 model, is very different: a large recess for the clip is milled into the titanium, so that the clip only protrudes slightly above the normal height of handle scales. Without the clip, the knife handle is 13 mm (0.5 in.) thick, and with the clip just 15 mm (0.6 in.). Thanks to the recess, you can

ALWAYS WITH YOU: THE CLIP | 8

Photos: Böker

Retractable HWAY clip on the Lion Steel ROK. The button on the front presses the clip out.

barely feel the clip in your palm even when holding the knife very firmly. However, neither this recessed clip nor the HWAY system could become established on the market, and they remain curiosities.

Clip in a milled recess on the WE Knife 901

8 | ALWAYS WITH YOU: THE CLIP

The different clips are the result of modified production and handle-mounting techniques, different requirements regarding accessibility and discreet carrying, and, of course, unique preferences in terms of design and aesthetic.

CHAPTER 9
LAWFUL WORK-AROUNDS: TWO-HANDED KNIVES AND SLIP JOINTS

While one-handed knives were developed for their practical function and usefulness, the existence of modern two-handed knives and slip joints without locking systems is primarily down to legal constraints. From a purely functional point of view, there is no reason to forgo the benefits of one-handed usage or a locking system.

In several nations, one-handed practical folding knives are restricted by law. For example, in Germany "folding knives that lock by one hand" are banned to carry in public areas unless you have a "legal reason" for a "generally recognized purpose" (see chapter 11). In the first years after this restriction came into force, the vague "legal reason" caused an increased demand for alternative solutions. Above all, German gun owners, who upon infringement of the Weapons Act could lose their gun license, pay fastidious attention to observing the law and therefore prefer the legal-to-carry two-handed knives.

"On the high seas and in court, we are in God's hands."

–Old saying–

To simplify things, we generally speak of one-handed knives, but Section 42a of the German Weapons Act specifies "folding knives that lock by one hand." Therefore, the solution for the problem is a knife that no longer has either of these characteristics. If you give a knife user the choice of their knife being either one-handed or lockable, the majority would favor a lockable knife for reasons of safety. And so, knives were created that fulfill all the criteria of a practical folding knife, with the exception of one-handed usage.

Opposite: Two-handed knives such as the Müller Liner-Lock Gent are not affected by bans of one-handed knives.

9 | LAWFUL WORK-AROUNDS: TWO-HANDED KNIVES AND SLIP JOINTS

Photos: Böker

After carrying of one-handed knives was restricted in Germany, Böker brought out a two-handed model (*bottom image*) of the popular flipper Turbine.

Two-handed models were now made based on popular one-handed knives. They had a traditional nail nick instead of a blade lifter or a flipper. Some of these two-handed models were given the suffix "42" in reference to the relevant paragraph of the law. Today, the suffix "free" is normally used.

Today, modern two-handed knives are primarily found in brands that strongly focus on European markets, above all Germany. For international brands, they are generally only produced when particular one-handed knives are popular and in demand on the German market, so that manufacturing a two-handed knife is worth it. In recent years, the demand is noticeably increasing again, which is said to primarily be due to the fear that laws may be restricted again.

To be 100% certain that a two-handed knife will comply with the German legislation, it's not enough to simply omit the blade lifter and the flipper; you also have to consider other details (see opposite page). The important thing is that the blade does not have any feature that would allow it to be opened one-handed (e.g., a blade lifter). Therefore, a nail nick should be far forward on the blade (i.e., not where the thumb touches it). It should also have a small and narrow shape, so that if you try to open it with one hand, your thumb will have no purchase. Furthermore, when closed, the blade should protrude as little as possible from the handle.

Some designers come up with further special features. The Linerlock Gent model from Müller features a

Modern two-handed knives: The Linerlock Gent from Müller and Titan Sepp from Oberland Arms

BKA AND TWO-HANDED KNIVES

A weapons legislation assessment by the German Federal Criminal Police Office (Bundeskriminalamt or BKA) (file no. So11–5164.01-Z-269) indicates how to design a two-handed knife that truly complies with the German legislation. In the assessment, the Foxtrot Two Outdoor by Pohl Force was graded as "lockable with one hand" despite not having a blade lifter. The German Federal Criminal Police Office determined that the knife could be opened with one hand "even without special skills or practice" on account of the very pronounced nail nick and the blade spine protruding far out of the handle, even when closed.

This type of thinking was elaborated on in an assessment of the Titan Sepp by Oberland Arms (file no. So13-5164.01-Z-530): "Since the closed blade does not allow the tips of the thumb and index finger enough space for the so-called pinch grip, the knife must be opened with two hands."

The note "without special skills or practice" is important. It indicates that for a knife to be considered two-handed, the user should not even hit on the idea of using the nail notch instead of the blade lifter to one-handedly open the knife with their thumb.

9 | LAWFUL WORK-AROUNDS: TWO-HANDED KNIVES AND SLIP JOINTS

The blade lifter on the Mike Five from Pohl Force can be unscrewed. The screw hole can be sealed with a small grub screw.

half-stop of the type familiar from slip joints. At 90°, the detent ball slips into a second slight notch. That not only provides additional safety when closing the knife, but also supports the knife's classification as a legislation-compliant two-handed knife. It's not possible to one-handedly open the knife by using any tricks. Nonetheless, in order to avoid unnecessary discussions with the police, it's sensible to have something in writing in your back pocket. For that reason, Oberland Arms paid for its Titan Sepp to be confirmed as conforming to Section 42a through an assessment by the German Federal Criminal Police Office—and you can carry this document with you (e.g., as a PDF on your smartphone).

UNSCREWING THE BLADE LIFTER

A quick look at knife catalogs reveals an almost unimaginable variety of modern one-handed knives in all shapes, sizes, and price classes. There are relatively few two-handed knives on the market. However, models with a traditional-style blade lifter often have the option of simply unscrewing the lifter. A former marketing manager from Benchmade used to call it "Germanizing the knife," because it's something that only German knife owners practice.

Some manufacturers deliberately plan the optional unscrewing of the blade lifter during the design and development process for new models. "For that reason, we even enclose the corresponding tools with many of our knives, so that buyers can at least temporarily remove the thumb pin," says Böker, which is based in Solingen. "It allows them as responsible citizens to decide for themselves how they want to use their knives."

A widespread book on weapons legislation in Germany presents the opinion that a knife could still be a one-handed knife in the legal sense despite the unscrewed blade lifter, because the blade lifter could be "attached with a few movements of the hands." This opinion is both contrary to all reason and legally questionable.

First, ownership of a one-handed knife is not prohibited in Germany, only carrying such a knife in public spaces without a legitimate interest. When you are out, if you don't also have the unscrewed blade lifter together with the knife, the legal impact of carrying a one-handed knife can no longer apply. It would be completely legal to screw the blade lifter back on at home. The notion that someone would unscrew a blade lifter and then carry it together with the knife, a Torx screwdriver, and the extremely small screw, in order to screw them back together while out so they have the speed benefit of a one-handed knife, is simply absurd.

Furthermore, Section 42a of the German Weapons Act does not define a specific form of construction but literally mentions the function of being lockable with one hand. Correspondingly, the German Federal Criminal Police Office also recorded (page 197) that to categorize a knife as a one-handed knife, it's not decisive if a blade lifter is mounted or not, but, rather, whether for the knife in question, "the opening and closing of the blade is possible with one hand." If that is no longer the case for a former one-handed knife with a detached blade lifter, then the criteria required by the German Federal Criminal Police Office are fulfilled.

Even renowned Swiss company Victorinox also has a modern two-handed knife in its range in the form of the Hunter Pro Alox.

9 | LAWFUL WORK-AROUNDS: TWO-HANDED KNIVES AND SLIP JOINTS

Two-handed knives such as the Walther BWK7, are usually equipped with a traditional nail nick.

It's generally very easy to unscrew a thumb pin. For some models—for example, Benchmade knives—you can immediately tell that it's a screw. An unscrewed thumb pin generally leaves behind a hole with an approximately 2mm (0.08-in.) diameter. As a rule, it barely affects the optical appearance, and dust and dirt can easily be cleaned from it because the screw thread is not in the hole but on the respective two halves of the thumb pin.

However, it's a different story for thumb disks. The open screw hole in the back of the blade is a trap for dust and dampness of all kinds. You risk the blade rusting from the inside. It's only in rare cases that a manufacturer supplies a grub screw to cover this hole after the knife leaves the factory.

Very often, the thumb pins are not just screwed in place but also secured with a lot of Loctite. If you feel a clear resistance when unscrewing a thumb pin, you need to first make the Loctite fluid by heating it with a hairdryer. Otherwise, you run the risk of destroying the screwhead. For knives where the thumb pin is also the stop pin (see page 57), they should not be removed. Depending on the locking system, the blade may no longer be able to safely lock without the pin.

Photo: Real Steel

MODERN SLIP JOINTS

There are also modern knives that forego the locking system instead of one-handed operation (some even have neither one-handed operation nor a locking system). Just like with a traditional Swiss Army Knife, only one spring presses against the blade and holds it in position for light cutting work. In modern designs, you may also find a system of double detent balls instead of a spring.

In Germany, on the topic of slipjoint knives, there is an explanatory assessment by the German Federal Criminal Police Office from which it's clear that for the "locking" criteria, there must be a mechanism that activates a "mechanical locking device" when the blade opens, and this locking device must be released when closing the blade. A blade that can be closed solely by placing pressure on the blade spine does not fulfill these criteria (file no. SO13–51654.01– Z-524).

Many modern slip joints have been deliberately created for specific legal situations. For the decidedly restrictive weapons legislation in Great Britain, the famous UK Pen Knife was developed by Spyderco. These days, some knives have neither one-handed operation nor a locking system. They're designed for users who want to be 100% on the safe side of the law.

The Real Steel Solis is a slipjoint: The blade does not lock but is held open by spring pressure. As a result, it's not street legal in most nations.

9 | LAWFUL WORK-AROUNDS: TWO-HANDED KNIVES AND SLIP JOINTS

LAWFUL WORK-AROUNDS: TWO-HANDED KNIVES AND SLIP JOINTS

The essential question of "Locking system or not?" is always a question of where the knife is to be used. For a fine gentleman's knife that is only occasionally used, and when it is, it's probably only to open an envelope, the lack of a locking system is less noticeable than on a knife that is used for robust cutting and carving. If you cut with a pull movement, all is well when using a slip joint. However, if you cut with a pushing movement and the tip of the knife meets with resistance or if you cant the blade while cutting, then pressure is no longer exerted directly on the cutting edge but from different directions. Eventually, the pressure in the spring or the detent ball is no longer enough to keep the knife open, so that the blade folds in and any fingers that are in the way get injured.

There are some models with very strong back springs, which provide quite a lot of holding force or, rather, a lot of stay, as American knife enthusiasts would say. However, the majority of slip joints on the market are designed for small and fine cutting jobs. If you want to work forcefully or carve, then a knife with a locking system is a better choice.

Opposite and left: The Böker Plus Caracal is one of the rare models that are available both as a lockable knife and a slipjoint.

9 | LAWFUL WORK-AROUNDS: TWO-HANDED KNIVES AND SLIP JOINTS

Modern slip joints are found increasingly frequently (Real Steel Luna). In contrast, two-handed knives are rare on the market (Elite Force EF170 · Real Steel H6 Free · SteelTac No. 2). However, even on some one-handed knives, you can relatively easily unscrew the thumb pin (Benchmade Rift).

LAWFUL WORK-AROUNDS: TWO-HANDED KNIVES AND SLIP JOINTS | **9**

Photo: Sharp by Coop

CHAPTER 10

TECHNOLOGY AND PHILOSOPHY: THE TYPES OF STEEL

Steel isn't just steel—you could write whole books on this topic. This chapter is not intended to be too theoretical, but a basic knowledge is useful in assessing the steel quality and, with it, the price/performance ratio of knives. Manufacturers often use the type of steel to justify significantly higher prices.

As a buyer with a basic knowledge of steel, you can make a well-founded judgment as to whether the price demanded is justified on the basis of the steel used. However, the expectations on steel have increased somewhat in recent years: in the 2000s, 154CM steel and its Japanese counterpart ATS-34 were still considered to be high-performance steels, but today in the knife community they are regarded as midrange.

Some manufacturers, Spyderco is a good example, produce their bestsellers in a range of steels from which the purchaser can choose. Also in this case, knowledge is important in order to be able make a good choice. This chapter on metallurgic properties is intended

"A mind needs books like a sword needs a whetstone."

–Tyrian Lannister (Game of Thrones)–

to be understandable for lay people, and therefore, as one of my uni professors liked to say, it "has been simplified to the point of falsification."*

There are various systems for categorizing types of steel. They are generally determined by the location of the steel producer. For example, companies in the United States use the AISI system (American Iron and Steel Institute), which divides the different steel groups into numbered groups. For example, the numbers in the 400s are for stainless steels (420, 440C . . .). In Germany, they use the DIN material

---

*If you want to know the exact science of it, I recommend the book *Knife Engineering: Steel, Heat Treating and Geometry* by Larrin Thomas.

Opposite: **Powder steel is usually used for expensive folding knives: RWL-34 on the Down by knife maker Brian Tighe.**

10 | TECHNOLOGY AND PHILOSOPHY: THE TYPES OF STEEL

Photo: Ovako

Most steel is produced by smelting alloys.

number or *Werkstoffnummer* according to German industrial standards (1.4034, 1.4116, etc.), while in the Far East, they use abbreviations, which are derived from the components of the most important alloy elements (8Cr13MoV, 9Cr18MoV, etc.). The manufacturing companies sometimes have also come up with their own designations (Elmax, CruWear, etc.).

Depending on the classification system, the same type of steel can be known by different names (D2 = X153CrVMo12-1 = 1.2379 = Böhler K110). In this book, we use the name that is most common on the international market for the different types of steel.

Steel is an alloy of iron and carbon, as well as further elements. It's important to note that steel is only used as a raw material. For a good blade, you not only require good material but also the correct heat treating. Imagine it as bread dough: even if the mixture of ingredients is correct, it only turns into a delicious bread with the correct baking time at the right temperature. For steel, the so-called heat treatment is commonly known as tempering.

The hardness of the finished blade is stated in HRC (Hardness Rockwell Cone). To test it, a diamond cone is pressed into the steel, and it's measured how deep this cone goes. Some knife producers carry out this hardness test for every blade. The imprint left by the diamond is regarded as a seal of quality. As a rule of thumb, the harder the blade, the greater the ability to hold an edge, but also the more fragile it is.

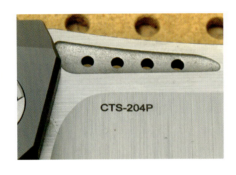

The type of steel used is generally lasered onto the back of the blade.

MASTER OF HEAT TREATMENT

A great deal of Buck's success can be traced back to a certain name: Paul Bos, who is famous for heat treatment in knife circles. Since doing a metalwork project at school, Paul has been fascinated with tempering and annealing steel. He has worked in this field his whole life, and his work with Buck goes back to the 1960s. For a few years, he was the owner of California's largest heat treatment plant until he got tired from the amount of work, and he sold the business in 1980.

Out of friendship to the Buck family and his love of knives, Paul Bos helped establish Buck's own heat treatment plant. In the 1980s, this cooperation led Paul to establish a new company for tempering blades on Buck's premises, in which he not only tempered knives from Buck but also from other producers and knife makers. In 2001, Bos sold the company in its entirety to Buck, and in 2010 he retired. Since then, "Paul Bos Heat Treating" has been operated as a division of Buck.

Paul Bos developed a special heat treatment procedure, in which the blades are first annealed, then cooled down, and then annealed again. In that way, he could get the best out of Buck's standard steel, 420HC. Buck's premium knives equipped with powder steel are subjected to a particularly elaborate heat treatment and are correspondingly labeled. "No one could match Paul's dedication to the art of heat treating knife blades," said Chuck Buck. "He is living proof to the conviction that it takes more than just using good steel for making a fine blade; it's what you do with the steel that makes the difference."

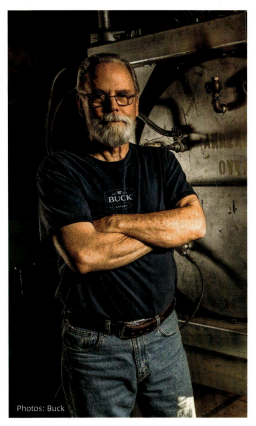

Paul Bos is an expert for heat treatment who is well respected in knife circles.

Buck uses the heat treatment by Paul Bos as a sign of quality.

It's a fine art to achieve the right compromise.

An important factor in selecting the hardness is the purpose of the blade; for instance, a low hardness of around 55 HRC is suitable for a really large bushcraft knife that has to endure stresses such as hacking.

Conversely, a pocketknife designed to hold an edge can be made much harder. For a stainless standard steel, a HRC of around 59 is considered a good hardness, while in contrast, modern powder steel exceeds 61 HRC.

For the heat treatment, the blade blanks that have been ground into shape are annealed and then chilled in a cold medium such as water or oil, or sometimes even compressed air. As a result, there is a change in the steel

THE BASIC TYPES OF KNIFE STEEL

	COMPOSITION	ADVANTAGES	DISADVANTAGES
Carbon steel, low-alloy steel (e.g., 1095, C75)	• With the exception of carbon, barely any alloy elements	• Blade can be sharpened to a very fine angle • Tough and resilient • Very easy to resharpen	• Rusts very quickly and quite badly • Less edge-holding ability
High-alloy tool steel (e.g., D2, A2, W2)	• Medium chrome content • Different percentages of special alloy elements	• Good edge-holding ability • Edge can be sharpened to a very fine angle • Can be annealed at very high temperatures • Resharpens rather well	• More or less stainless
Stainless steel (e.g., 440 C, N690, 14C28N)	• More than 13% chrome • Further alloy elements in different percentages	• Stainless • Resistant to wear and tear with increasing percentage of alloy elements	• Blade cannot be ground to a really fine angle • Less tough • Large, irregularly distributed carbides • With increasing percentage of alloy elements, harder to sharpen
Powder steel (e.g., S35VN, M390)	• Extremely high percentage of chrome* and other alloy elements * with the exception of powder-metallurgical tool steel	• Stainless • Cutting edge can be sharpened to a fine angle • Can be annealed at very high temperatures • Very high edge-holding ability • Very resistant to wear and tear • Small and more finely distributed carbides	• Difficult to sharpen

SHARPENING KNIVES

Sharpening knives is a topic in itself. The sharpening results depend on several factors:
- the level of wear and tear
- the type of steel
- the medium used for sharpening
- your own practical skills

Photo: Spyderco

While people who have good practical skills have a preference for freehand sharpening using the traditional benchstones, many people don't have the confidence and therefore choose a device with sharpening angles that can be set (*photo*: Spyderco Triangle Sharpmaker). Knives made using powder steel with high wear-resistant properties can barely be sharpened with normal stones—in this case it's best to use diamond stones. Addressing the topic of sharpening in the required detail would be too much for this book. However, numerous books have been dedicated to this topic. Recommended reading for beginners: *Knife Sharpening Made Easy* by Stefan Steigerwald and Peter Fronteddu.

structure: the blade is now very hard, but at the same time also very brittle. In order to reduce the danger of breakage, the blade is annealed—in a sense, it's baked a low temperature of approximately 500°F to 700°F. Only once the heat treatment has been completed does the steel have the right hardness and toughness.

For every type of steel, there is a maximum and a recommended hardness range. If, after heat treatment, this range is exceeded, the blade is prone to breakage. Therefore, for every steel alloy, a bespoke exact heat treatment is needed. The importance of the proper treatment is excellently illustrated in the knives made by Buck. For models that are not made in the Far East but in the USA, the company usually works with annealing specialist Paul Bos. Bos is famous for drawing out a considerable performance from 420HC, a steel that is actually a really basic metal (page 209).

The different properties of the steel alloys are produced either by adding further elements such as chrome, molybdenum, or vanadium to the iron during smelting or during the powder-metallurgical process (more on this later). Knife steel is categorized into four basic types based on their properties (see table on opposite page).

Traditional carbon steels are today mostly used for traditional pocket-knives— for example, the models from

TECHNOLOGY AND PHILOSOPHY: THE TYPES OF STEEL

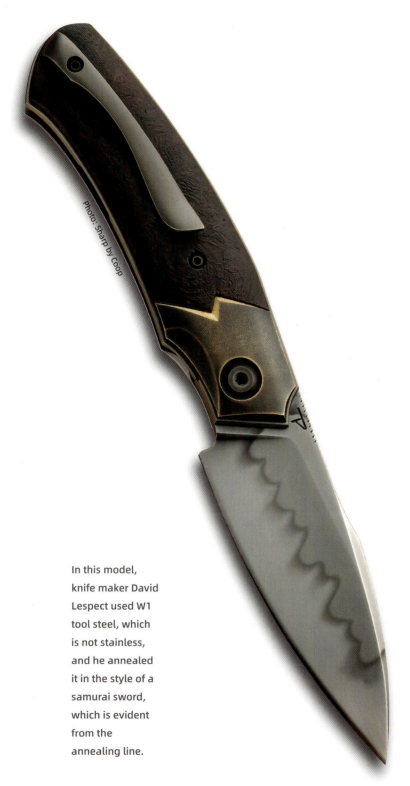

In this model, knife maker David Lespect used W1 tool steel, which is not stainless, and he annealed it in the style of a samurai sword, which is evident from the annealing line.

Opinel or Case—and due to their high tendency to rust are very seldom used for modern pocketknives. However, they are still used by knife makers generally to differentially hardened blades (for instance, on a samurai swords), and to create a visible annealing line (Hamon), which is not possible with high-alloy steels. It does not have any functional advantages over modern high-end steels but is intended for aficionados of traditional craftsmanship.

High-alloy tool steels, rather corrosion-resistant but not completely stainless, are also not preferred steels for folding knives, because compared to fixed knives, rust is a significantly bigger problem for pocketknives. These steels are used by knife makers predominantly for models for knife enthusiasts, who care well for such knives and generally keep them in glass show cases.

An exception is D2, which in recent years has been seen more and more often on modern folding knives. This steel is not expensive, is easy to work with, and has a high percentage of carbon (1.5%) and a relatively high percentage of chrome (11.5%). Therefore, D2 brings together many of the good properties of traditional carbon steel with a fairly high rust resistance.

Photo: Spyderco

SPECIAL ALLOYS

The basic principle of a practical folding knife is to be as effective as possible in a multitude of situations. Therefore, the steels used must have a more or less balanced mixture of the following properties: ability to hold an edge, rust resistance, resilience, and ability to be resharpened. However, for special purposes, you need alloys that are more stainless. For example, the knives in Spyderco's Salt line, which as the name suggests is designed for use in situations when you are constantly in contact with salt water, or water in general (e.g., fishing, diving, high-sea angling, but also surfing or canoe sports). Therefore, very stainless special alloys, such as H1, are used for these knives. H1 contains a lot of chrome, but only a small amount of carbon—it's replaced by larger amounts of nitrogen and copper.

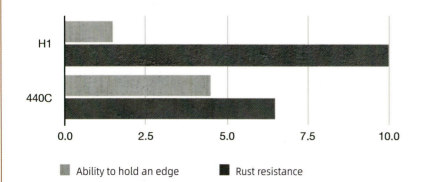

Compared to a standard steel, such as 440C, H1 is extremely stainless but has less ability to hold an edge.

STAINLESS STEEL

The vast majority of modern pocketknives have blades made of stainless steel with over 13% chrome. In addition, these steels also have a more or less high percentage of alloy elements. Since pocketknives are usually carried in trouser pockets and are constantly exposed to evaporated sweat, corrosion resistance is of great importance. Colloquially, corrosion-resistant steel is referred to as stainless (also inox). However, that is not technically correct and as a result leads to unrealistic expectations: essentially all knife steels will rust if exposed to constant, long-term damp conditions. Even the designation "stainless steel" is factually incorrect. Real rust-free stainless steels with high percentages of chrome and nickel, but a low percentage of carbon, are not sufficiently annealable and are therefore not suitable for blades. At best, they can be used for knife handles.

The range of stainless blade steels is huge. It starts from low-priced 420 steel and simple steel types such as 440A and 420HC and goes up to the high-end types, such as 154CM and VG10. The latter have a high percentage of alloy elements, which makes the steels resistant to wear and tear. Thus, they give the steel specific properties. However, the elements may react with each other, and therefore they need to be mixed very precisely to prevent the effect of one element being canceled out by another element.

Sadly, when making steel you cannot simply add x-amount of alloy elements and create a "super steel." Although industrial steel production enormously progressed in the twentieth century, there are still two technical problems for stainless steel.

Iron, the main element in steel, can only bond with a limited number of alloy elements. Once the limit has been reached, everything else is excreted in the cooling phase after it has been

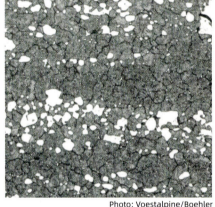

Carbides (*white*) are harder than the steel structure and arise when carbon bonds with other elements such as iron, chrome, or vanadium. This is a carbide-rich steel.

Photo: Voestalpine/Boehler

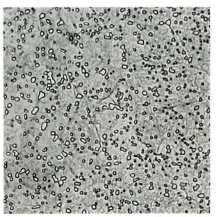

In comparison, here is a structure image of 12C27 steel by Sandvik. It also contains carbides, but they are much smaller and more evenly distributed.

Photo: Sandvik

melted. If, when producing steel, you add too much carbon, it's expelled as graphite when cooling—and you do not create a good steel, but a cast iron that cannot be annealed.

The second problem for stainless steel is the too-big and irregular carbides. They are formed during the melting process, when certain elements such as chrome, vanadium, molybdenum, and tungsten bond with carbon. The microscopic bonds are extremely hard—much harder than the surrounding steel matrix. For that reason, they increase the edge-holding ability, which is a positive. When the melted steel cools down, the small carbides form clumps. If they become too

THE ALLOY ELEMENTS AND THEIR EFFECTS

Carbon (C)
+ increases hardness, ability to hold an edge, tensile strength, and resistance to wear and tear
− large amounts increase susceptibility to breakage

Chrome (Cr)
+ makes corrosion resistance; increases hardness, tensile strength, resistance to wear and tear
− reduces resilience

Molybdenum (Mo)
+ increases hardness, annealability, pressure resistance, and machinability; makes it more rustproof; ensures a finer steel structure

Vanadium (V)
+ increases resilience and resistance to wear and tear, ensures a finer steel structure

Manganese (Mn)
+ increases annealability, resistance to wear and tear, and tensile strength
− large amounts increase susceptibility to breakage

Nitrogen (N)
+ can replace carbon to a certain extent–has a similar effect but is not susceptible to corrosion

Cobalt (Co)
+ increases hardness, resilience, and thermal stability; has a strengthening effect on other elements

Niobium (Nb)
+ increases resilience, makes more corrosion resistant, ensures a finer steel structure

Tungsten (W)
+ increases resilience and annealability

Nickel (Ni)
+ increases resilience, hardness, and machinability

Silicon (Si)
+ increases resilience

Phosphor (P)
+ increases machinability and hardness
− large amounts increase susceptibility to breakage

Sulfur (S)
+ increases machinability
− large amounts reduce hardness

Copper (Cu)
+ Makes it more corrosion resistant

big (on a microscopic level), the matrix can no longer hold them, and if such a clump of carbides is located right on the cutting edge of a knife blade, it breaks free under stress. Where this happens, longer, microscopic cracks may arise.

As a result of this carbide problem, stainless steel cannot be ground to extremely fine blades with small cutting angles, because the risk of the carbides breaking away is too great. Therefore, for stainless steel, a moderately robust cutting angle of approximately 40° is recommended. Steels that are both very resistant to wear and tear and rustproof with a high proportion of carbides are also difficult to resharpen.

POWDER STEEL

Powder steel was developed as a solution to the problem concerning large carbides and the limitations of the alloy elements. Steels made using the powder-metallurgical procedure are not melted but go through HIP (hot isostatic pressing). In this procedure, no carbide clumps are formed.

It all starts with metal powder. For it, a steel melt with the desired alloy components is produced. Before the molten steel can cool, it's sprayed through small ceramic nozzles into a chamber filled with nitrogen. By doing so, a hard jet of nitrogen gas atomizes the molten metal into particles with

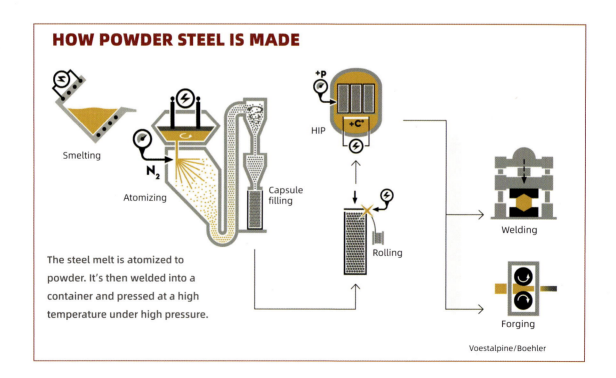

HOW POWDER STEEL IS MADE

Smelting · Atomizing · Capsule filling · HIP · Rolling · Welding · Forging

The steel melt is atomized to powder. It's then welded into a container and pressed at a high temperature under high pressure.

Voestalpine/Boehler

Photo: Sandrin

TUNGSTEN CARBIDE BLADES

Tungsten carbides are formed from the tungsten-carbon bond and are used in the production of carbide metals. Extremely hard tungsten carbide is well known as a material for drills, wire cutters, glass breakers, and knife sharpeners. For a long time, it was not considered possible to use it for knife blades due to its susceptibility to breakage that comes with the hardness. However, Italian company Sandrin has found a suitable alloy. The exact recipe remains a secret, but essentially a mixture of wolfram carbide powder and carbon is sintered at 1,400°C to 2,000°C. In the process, a very fine and extremely solid molecule structure is formed. By the end of the procedure, the blades have a hardness of a proud 71 HRC and, according to the manufacturer, are considerably more resilient than ceramic, if not as resilient as steel.

The Sandrin blade achieves an edge-holding ability that is far superior to commercial steels. In the test by MESSER MAGAZIN (*The Knife Magazine*), it was recorded that the blade stayed sharp for at least twice as long as M390 powder steel, which is already very resilient to wear and tear. However, the tungsten carbide blades can only be sharpened with diamond or sintered ruby; conventional stone sharpeners or ceramic sharpeners have no chance.

approximately 0.1 mm (0.004-in.) diameter. These tiny particles cool and become rigid when falling. They land as a fine metal powder at the bottom of the chamber. The cooling happens so fast that there is no time for the alloy elements to separate, and the carbides also remain tiny.

The fine metal powder is poured under vacuum into a stainless-steel cylinder, which is welded closed. It then goes through a hot isostatic procedure. The sealed cylinder is pressed under a heat of 2,100°F and a pressure of 1,000 bar. As a result, the powder is sintered, or baked solid, so to speak. A solid block of steel is formed.

The advantages of powder steel are a larger percentage of alloy elements,

TECHNOLOGY AND PHILOSOPHY: THE TYPES OF STEEL

Photo: Sharp by Coop

Knife maker Richard Rogers used powder-metallurgical Damasteel for the blade of the Axiom.

no air pockets or impurities, and also a very fine distribution of carbides. Powder steel is more resilient than conventional stainless steels, is considerably more resistant to wear and tear, and keeps its cutting properties better. On the other hand, it's also significantly more expensive and harder to sharpen.

DAMASCUS STEEL

Among knife enthusiasts, Damascus steel is a very popular material. Two or three different types of steel or iron are welded together by heating in the forge and hammering. The name "Damascus steel" originates from the Syrian city of Damascus, which in the Middle Ages was a central hub for swords and weapons. Before the Migration Period (also known as the Barbarian Invasions), some European armorer or other had the great idea of welding together several alternate layers of soft iron and hard steel (or softer and harder steel) to achieve a simultaneously elastic and hard blade. Essentially, it's an enhancing procedure. If you acid-treat smooth polished Damascus steel, the layers are shown as a pattern because the parts that are richer in carbon react more to the acid and become dark.

Depending on the forging technique, you can create specific patterns, which in the early Middle Ages probably also had magical meanings. At a time in which solidly forged steel was almost unaffordable, Damascus steel represented a high point of the technology, which was of course vastly superior to the majority of sword blades. As good steel became more affordable, Damascus steel grew technologically outdated. Nevertheless, Damascus steel remains a legend, and with the boom in handcrafted custom knives, it has also become popular in the world of knives.

In terms of cutting performance, Damascus steel has no advantage over modern types of steel. However, it still has its special mystique, and the fascinating appearance of its patterns continues to delight. From a practical point of view, its beauty is also unfortunately a disadvantage, because if you scratch such a blade when working, you are more annoyed than if you were working with a mono steel. No wonder that knives made of Damascus steel are often not used and are immediately put in a glass showcase.

At the start of the 1980s, the invention of stainless Damascus steel by knife makers Friedrich Schneider and Richard Hehn was seen as a technological innovation. Normally, stainless steels cannot be fire-forged, because when heated the chrome in the steel reacts with the oxygen in the air and forms an oxide layer on the surface that prevents welding.

The solution, which Schneider and Hehn thought up, was as simple as it was innovative: stainless-steel sheets are welded into a tin can, then the air is sucked from it and the tin is sealed. Therefore, the steel package in the tin is in a vacuum. The whole tin is heated and can now be fire-forged.

A special type of stainless Damascus steel was developed in the late 1990s by the company of the same name, Damasteel. It's produced using powder metallurgy and therefore has all the advantages of powder steel. Two different kinds of steel powder are poured into a steel cylinder. The trick is not to mix the two powders

Damascus steel is produced in various patterns (Accomplice by Steven Skiff).

Photo: Sharp by Coop

The M1, designed by Greg Lightfoot, was produced in series by CRKT. The blades were coated in different colors, using titanium nitride.

too much when pouring them in but to leave them as layers. The mixture then undergoes the vacuum and HIP procedures. Damasteel is a very expensive material that is seldom used for knives that are serially produced.

For modern folding knives, Damascus steel is produced in specialist workshops and larger industrial plants. Larger steel sheets are rolled together under heat, and the whole rolling line is placed in a vacuum or a protective atmosphere. Damascus steel with a cutting core is particularly popular for modern knives. The core layer consists of a stainless steel such as VG 10 or, for cheaper models, 8Cr13MoV. Several layers of stainless Damascus steel are rolled on both sides. This special Damascus steel is often called by its Japanese name, Suminagashi, or also San Mai Damascus.

COATINGS AND FINISHINGS

The blades of numerous pocketknives on the market are coated, with just the cutting bevel uncovered. In addition to appearances, the manufacturers also take functional purposes into consideration when applying a coating. First, the blade should be protected against corrosion. Very smooth coatings, such as Teflon (PTFE), ensure that the blade slides more easily through the material to be cut. In contrast, very hard coatings, such as DLC, should protect the blade from scratches.

Fixed-blade knives sometimes also have thicker powder coatings based on epoxide. However, such a coating would interfere with the mechanisms on a pocketknife. They have extremely thin, hard coatings that are only a few micrometers thick.

Coatings are applied in different ways: by spraying, vapor deposition (CVD = chemical vapor deposition), galvanization, or physical vapor evaporation (PVD). Depending on the coating, there is a heat treatment, which permanently binds the coating to the steel surface.

Over the course of time, knife producers have tried various coating methods, of which only a few have become established. Coatings can be divided into three basic types:

- Chemical coatings: Chemicals are used to oxidize the surface of the blade; for example, black oxide.
- Polymer coatings: They include Teflon, Dura-Coat, Gun-Kote, and Cera-Kote (with a ceramic component).
- Hard coatings: They include titanium nitride (TiN), titanium carbon nitride (TiCN) or titanium aluminum nitride (TiAlN), and DLC (Diamond Like Carbon) on graphite bases or chrome compounds, such as chrome nitride (CrN).

While the surface of traditional carbon steels is case hardened using polishing methods, such as the traditional Solinger Blau Pließten (blue polishing), and in doing so a certain level of corrosion resistance is achieved, there are two reasons for applying a finish to modern wear-resistant and stainless knife steels: the cut is noticeably smoother thanks to an incredibly smooth finish, and second, the finish enhances its appearance. Depending on the desired appearance, the surface is satined (an effect created with a fine sanding belt and polishing brushes) to give a more or less finely polished surface. Usually, it's satined at a 90° angle to the longitudinal axis, but you

The CRKT Anubis, designed by Allen Elishewitz, has a gray glass bead-blasted blade or black titanium nitride coating.

10 | TECHNOLOGY AND PHILOSOPHY: THE TYPES OF STEEL

In this example, the main bevel and the blade side have been satined in two different directions.

also often find different angles that lend the blade a dynamic appearance. For high-quality knives, different types of satining are often combined.

Sometimes, the surfaces are also blasted. A matte-gray finish is produced by sandblasting with corundum particles. However, the sandblasting makes the surface very rough, and as a result, it's more susceptible to rust. Blasting with round glass beads also creates a matte-gray surface but damages the steel less; depending on the steel, the glass bead blasting can also have a case hardening effect on the surface. However, scratches are particularly noticeable on blasted surfaces.

The so-called stonewash finish is also prevalent on knives. To create this finish, the workpiece is placed in a barrel machine together with abrasive particles in a process called barrel finishing. Depending on the size of the abrasive particles and the duration of the process, a more or less fine pattern of scratches, almost crystalline in appearance, is created. It not only looks cool but enjoys the benefit that it disguises small scratches that happen unavoidably during use.

In terms of functionality, stonewash is the most user-friendly finish. In order to achieve a darker appearance, you can acid-treat the metal (acid stonewash) or coat with hard coating (blackwash) before barrel finishing. These stonewashed alternatives create a special used look (page 224).

TYPES OF STEEL AND THEIR PROPERTIES

Many knife producers state the percentage of alloy elements found in the types of steel used. In order to be able to understand the blade properties from this information, some basic metallurgical knowledge is required.

Therefore, for all the most important steels on the market I've put together a graphic showing their ability to hold an edge, rustproof qualities, resilience, and ease of sharpening.

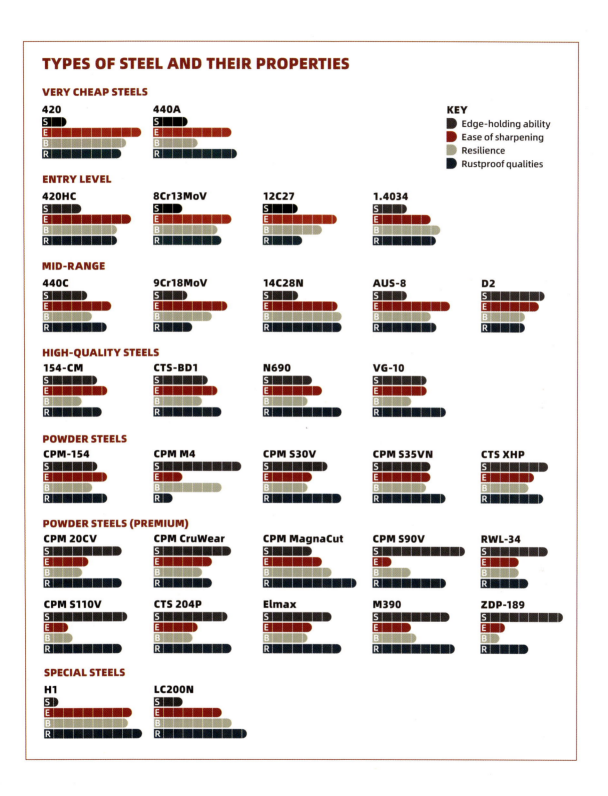

Blades with different types of stonewash finish: matte-gray acid stonewash (Prototyp SteelTac No.1) · PVD-coated stonewash (Fox M1) · blackwash (Böker Plus Field Folding knife) · light stonewash (Kershaw CQC-10K)

TECHNOLOGY AND PHILOSOPHY: THE TYPES OF STEEL | 10

Photo: Sharp by Coop

CHAPTER 11
POLITICS AND KNIFE BANS

In many nations around the world, there are legal restrictions against pocketknives. It's important to understand the political background of such restrictions. While the following pages illustrate the example of Germany, these mechanisms are nearly the same in every constitutional democracy. In the US, the AKTI (American Knife and Tool Institute, www.akti.org) fights for the civil right to own and carry knives and provides up-to-date information on knife laws.

THE BACKGROUND OF KNIFE BANS

In Germany, pocketknives other than switchblades weren't restricted until 2003. Since then, butterfly knives (balisongs) and gravity knives have been banned, and knife bans have become increasingly stricter over the past twenty years. But instead of consequently targeting offenders, such knife bans are not a solution for everyday criminality because the police and justice departments "have been economized to breaking point for decades. Sufficient staffing and modern equipment are lacking," according to the senior prosecutor in Berlin, Ralph Knispel, in his book *Rechtsstaat am Ende (End of the State of Law)*. He complains of the "failure of the state of law, which has long been incapable of meeting its task of maintaining public safety."

He believes that more police and consistent punishment are needed to solve the problem, but it appears that appetite is lacking in this regard both for ideological and financial reasons. Knife bans are a welcome diversionary tactic, since, although they don't solve the problem, they don't cost anything. Knife enthusiasts can sometimes be seen as scapegoats.

"Where injustice becomes law, resistance becomes duty."
–Motto of the civil rights movement

Opposite: **Even valuable pieces of art, such as this pocketknife by David Sharp, are a thorn in the side of many politicians.**

11 | POLITICS AND KNIFE BANS

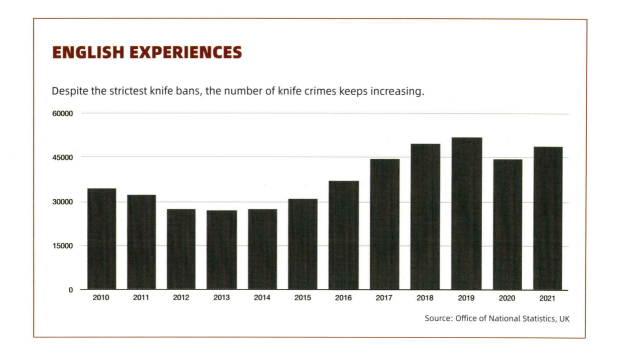

ENGLISH EXPERIENCES

Despite the strictest knife bans, the number of knife crimes keeps increasing.

Source: Office of National Statistics, UK

Unfortunately, there are still no long-term statistics in Germany from which it can be determined how the crime rate develops in connection with knives. In contrast, in England and Wales this trend has been statistically recorded for many years. They have extremely strict knife laws, and by the mid-twentieth century, there was practically nowhere in English cities where you were permitted to carry a harmless Swiss Army Knife.

But despite all the bans and media campaigns, the number of crimes involving knives continued to rise. The year 2019 saw the highest rate in over fifty years. After a pandemic-induced drop in 2020, the knife crimes were noticeably increasing again.

ONE-HANDED KNIVES AS THE ENEMY

Typical for a restriction without reason or any evidence is the ban of one-handed knives in Germany's public spaces in 2008 (see page 195). Responsible was Berlin's then-Senator of the Interior Ehrhart Körting. According to senior prosecutor Ralph Knispel, "The majority of crimes occur [in Berlin] and that is where the fewest are solved." In 2007, a crime that attracted much attention was committed. At the beach in Tegel, Berlin, an argument escalated and three youths attacked a father. A twenty-three-year-old man who wanted to mediate was stabbed from behind with an already-banned butterfly knife. The

POLITICS AND KNIFE BANS | 11

Photo: UK Homeoffice

Photo: Essex Police

Above: "Knife-free" posters featured "Sonny." *Left*: In Great Britain, amnesty bins for knives are frequently plundered.

11 | POLITICS AND KNIFE BANS

Photo: CRKT

Even rescue knives are included in 42a. The authorities only rarely show discretion or leniency.

perpetrator, Erol A. (age seventeen), not only was known to the police but also had previous convictions. At the age of fifteen, he had already attacked a person with a butcher's knife.

Because of this crime and the sustained high rate of criminality, the Senator was under pressure. However, instead of employing more police, he chose a scapegoat: Körting deliberately painted the one-handed knife as the enemy. "People who own such knives carry them consciously as a weapon or use them as a threatening gesture," he claimed. He added that a ban would be sensible, "if only to dry out the market for knives."

Politicians ignored all counterarguments, even ones coming from the police experts. "Körting's planned ban is wrong, excessive, and not practical," emphasized the then-chairperson of the German police trade union, Konrad Freiberg. He predicted it would be useless and believed that the threat of punishment for unpermitted knife carrying is devoid of purpose compared to the criminalization of violent crimes—instead, hundreds and thousands of citizens would be criminalized. However, most German politicians were open to tightening the weapons legislation, and therefore Körting's demands became a proposed law.

Körting was able to convince the committee of the interior that one-handed knives are particularly dangerous and that "for many youths with a propensity to violence, they have taken on the cult status of the prohibited but-

terfly knife." It's a claim that couldn't and still can't be proven. Just before the vote in the Bundestag (German parliament), the last doubters were brought into line with a cleverly edited "video of proof" of an allegedly fatal knife attack. After the video was viewed, the legislation was passed.

In this way, carrying "cutting and thrust weapons [and] knives with a blade that can be locked with one hand (one-handed knives) or fixed knives with a blade length of over 12 cm" in public was prohibited. Although you can buy and own the knives completely legally, you may not carry them in a public space. This legislation was a radical break from the previous legal principles, which affected only weapons but not utility knives.

To avoid the predictable chaos, at least on paper, exemption clauses for "socially acceptable use" were included. Accordingly, the carry ban did not apply if you can provide a "legal reason." As per the German Weapons Act*, you have an interest if you are carrying your knife in connection with your job, in accordance with tradition, for sport, or to serve a generally recognized purpose. This list is neither conclusive nor exclusive. The law lists as examples for legal reasons to the weapons legislation "picnics, mountain climbing, gardening, rescue, cultivating traditions, hunting, and fishing."

---

* Can be read at www.verwaltungsvorschriften-im-internet.de.

Totally imaginary film scenes, such as the knife fight in *Rebel without a Cause*, have had a lasting negative influence on how society regards pocketknives.

11 | POLITICS AND KNIFE BANS

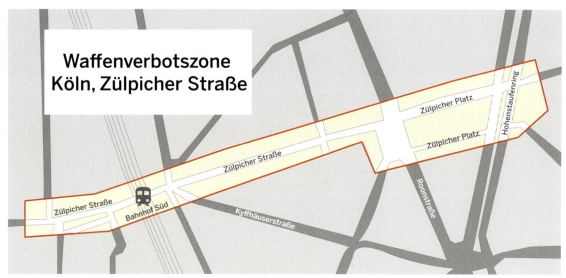

Photos: Polizei NRW

German federal states may allow the local municipalities to establish prohibition zones according to their own discretion.

If you regard a one-handed knife as a tool and deploy it for socially acceptable purposes, then it corresponds both to the text of the law and the explanations accompanying the law. Therefore, the point of the spirit and letter of the law is not whether you need a one-handed knife for a purpose permitted by the authorities, but, rather, if you are using it in a socially acceptable manner (i.e., what you are using it for).

After the adoption of Section 42a, Körting still made assurances that it was about "having legal grounds to confiscate a knife during police operations that were already being carried out anyway," and not "to carry out knife checks among law-abiding citizens." However, in practice, the authorities generally treat the paragraph a lot more restrictively, and knife users don't have legal certainty.

As feared by police expert Freiberg, the law has resulted in the criminalization of citizens. Accordingly, even the exceptions stated in the law, such as for work and sport, are often not recognized. The vaguely phrased "for generally recognized purpose" is often interpreted negatively for the person affected. A judgment from the Higher Regional Court in Stuttgart is notorious: a one-handed knife in the side door of a car, "so that in the case of an emergency the safety belt can be cut," does not serve any "generally recognized purpose" (File no. 4 Ss 137/11).

If you are stopped by the police and have a one-handed knife with you, you can expect a monetary fine. In practice, the police have some power of discretion. Many accept a believably presented justified interest. As experience shows, the probability of an average citizen, whom the police don't notice, being stopped by the police is relatively low. In my years as of the editor of *Weapons: Internal Market*, many readers have told me things along the lines of "I've never been stopped by the police, and I think the risk of it is rather low."

TERROR ATTACKS AND KNIFE BANS

In 2024, Germany was shocked by three major terror attacks — two of them executed with knives. On the morning of May 31, members of a German

Photo: Police NRW

After the 2024 terror attack in Solingen, the Ministry of Interior for the federal state Northrhine started the multilingual poster campaign "better without a knife."

counter-jihad organization set up their information booth on the market square of Mannheim. Although the scene was watched by several police officers, they were suddenly attacked by Afghan refugee Suleiman A. with a large knife. He wanted to stop opponents of Islam, prosecutors said. In the 25 seconds until Suleiman A. was stopped with a non-lethal shot, he severely injured six people. Twenty-nine-year-old Police Officer Rouven L. was stabbed in the neck and died three days later of his injuries.

On the evening of August 2, the citizens of the famous German knife-making town Solingen were celebrating the 650th anniversary of their town. At an open air concert, Syrian refugee Issa al H. took out a large knife and stabbed into the crowd. Three people were killed, and eight people severely injured. Issa al H. was caught a day later.

Both terror attacks clearly showed that knife bans don't stop such crimes. Suleiman A. carried a large outdoor knife in his backpack. Issa al H. took a cooking knife with a six-inch-blade from the kitchen of the shelter with him. All these knives exceeded the 4.7-inch-limit for fixed blades on public areas, demonstrating that many criminals ignore knife bans. But after the 2024 terror attacks, the German government preferred to focus on knife restrictions and new knife bans for law-abiding citizens.

In November 2024, the German government passed bills calling for more knife bans. The already existing ban of switchblades became even more restricted (see page 172). The prohibition against carrying weapons at public events was extended to all kind of knives. Public events can mean many things: you are no longer allowed to carry a pocketknife while watching a movie in cinemas. German federal states now are allowed to declare all areas with public traffic prohibition zones where all knives are banned. This includes school surroundings, market places, public transport, and more.

The new knife laws include exceptions for legal reasons, but the former experiences (see page 231) show that authorities will execute this rather strictly, and even law-abiding citizens will have no legal certainty.

Again, the knife bans of 2024 not based on reason or evidence, but a result of bias, ideology, political opportunism, and despair of terror attacks. Looking at this, knife bans are not only useless but an unnecessary diversionary tactic.

A POCKETKNIFE POPULIST?

Although many politicians favor general knife bans for law-abiding citizens before reasonable actions against criminals, there are also few politicians with sensible opinions. Hubert Aiwanger (Freie Wähler Party) succinctly got to the heart of the political discussion about carrying knives. In October 2019, as the Bavarian vice minister president, he criticized the planned knife bans, saying, "I'm convinced that Bavaria and Germany would be safer if every decent man and every decent woman would be allowed to have a knife in their pocket, and if we locked up re-offending criminals. That would be the right way." He expressed incomprehension that, on the one hand, they were discussing pocketknife prohibition in public places, but it was accepted with a shoulder shrug that "people who have committed crimes and offenses causing bodily harm" can move around freely.

Reactions from political opponents promptly followed. "Serious security policy does not mix with pocketknife populists," said Horst Arnold (Free Voters). Katharina Schulze (The Greens Party) was indignant, saying, "His recommendation to carry around self-defense knives in daily life is not only stupid, but also dangerous." The police have the monopoly on the legitimate use of force; "Those who call on citizens to arm themselves are advocating the law of the jungle." This "notion of conflict resolution from the Middle Ages" is "extremely embarrassing."

Despite the uproar, Aiwanger stood by what he said and maintained his position: "The constant tightening of weapons legislation for law-abiding citizens misses the point. Those who advocate pocketknife bans and think that they will stop violent crimes are extremely embarrassing." He added that the claim he would call on people to arm themselves was "maliciously and deliberately misinterpreted." He said he was simply against any further tightening of weapons legislation, which in Germany is already strict anyway. He believed that the discussed knife ban in public places was going in the wrong direction and would cause problems for law-abiding citizens, adding that "we need to prosecute violent criminals in a targeted manner instead."

Hubert Aiwanger took a stance against knife bans.

INDEX OF KEY WORDS

3-D milling	33, 67, 79
additional fuse	125, 127
aircraft aluminum	87
AISI (American Iron and Steel Institute)	207
alloy	208
alloying elements	215
aluminum	86f
American Tanto	95, 109
anchor	135
anodizing	88
anticorodal	87
assisted opener	173f
ATCF (Advanced Tactical Combat Folder)	25, 182
automatic knife	173f
axis lock	143f
axle bolt	159
back blade	93
back-lock	137f
backspacer	74, 186
ball-bearing lock	144
ball bearings	33, 154f, 169
barrel finish	222
Benchmade	143
blade axle	120, 131
blade bearings	154f
blade geometry	98f
blade length	29, 54, 111f
blade shape	93f
bolster lock	134
bolt-action lock	144
Bos, Paul	209, 211
Bowie	93
Boye Dent	138
bronze	154
Buck	209
Buck 110	27
button lock	148f
carabiner	189
carbide	215
carbon	84 f, 208
carbon steel	212
Carson, Kit	30
Chinese manufacturing	35f
chisel grind	108
clip	25, 179ff
clip point	93
CNC machines	30
coating	220
cold steel	139
combi grind	109
compression lock	145
copper shred	85
CRKT	36
CRKT M16	30
crossbar lock	145
crowned cut	106
cutting angle	98, 101, 111
cutting bevel thickness	100f
cutting properties	45, 98
Damasteel	220
deadbolt lock	146
deep-carry clip	50, 185
Demko, Andrew	140
DLC (Diamond-Like Carbon)	221
drop point	93
EDC (Every Day Carry)	15, 48
Emerson, Ernest	108, 160
ergonomics	66f
fiberglass	77f
finish	221f
flat grinding	106
Flick-It	23
flipper	30, 33, 166f, 175, 196
floating stop pin	57
force triangle	119, 131
frame lock	70, 129f
FRN (Fiberglass Reinforced Nylon)	77f
front flipper	169
front lock	137
G-10, G10	78f, 85
gap (at the root of the blade)	46, 120
Gibbs's Rule No. 9	18, 179
Glesser, Sal	23, 164, 180
grinding angle	101
grinding types	106
hardening	208, 211
Hawkbill	97
heat treatment	208
Hinderer, Rick	133
hollow grinding	106
HRC (Hardness Rockwell Cone)	208
IKBS (Ikoma Korth Ball Bearing System)	154
Ikoma, Flavio	117, 146, 154
Integral-Lock	129
Klecker-Lock	137
K-tip	95
lanyard	74
lanyard eyelet	74
LAWKS (Lake and Walker Safety)	125, 129
left-handed	108, 128, 145, 182
legitimate interest (WaffG)	230

APPENDIX

light metal 87
lightning-strike effect 85
liner 70, 77
liner lock 25, 118f
lock bar 131
locking liner 119, 126
locking spring 119, 126
Loctite 75, 200
main bevel (grinding) 99
material number 208
Mercator 185
micarta 79f
midlock 137
mid-tech knives 37
more socially adequate use
(Weapons Act) 230
MUDD folding knife 142
nail notch 195
nanoceramics 88
nested liner 119
oil 161
one-handed operation 153f
Onion, Ken 175
overstretch protection 133, 135
overtravel stop 133
Paragraph 42a, WaffG __ 173, 195f, 228ff
Persian blade shape 97
polished to zero 99, 106
powder steel 216
practical folding knives 9
price categories 35, 59
prohibition zones 232f
PVD (physical vapor deposition) 221
quality control 56
recessed flipper 171
Reeve, Chris 129, 135
Reeve Sebenza 129
Reverse Tanto 95
Richlite 82
Rockwell Hardness 208

saber grind 106
Salt line (Spyderco) 213
satin finish 222
Scandi grind 106
screws 75
serrated edge 104
sharpened crowbar 45
sharpening 104
sheepfoot 97
shoulders 100
sliding discs 33, 154
slipjoint 116, 201f
spear point 93
Speedsafe 175
spinewhack test 117
Spyderco 23, 144, 164, 180, 213
Spyderco Worker 23
stainless steel 214
standoffs 74
steel 86, 121, 129
steel properties 223
steel types 210
Steigerwald, Stefan 68, 126
stonewash finish 222
stop pin 55, 119, 200
subframe lock 134
Suminagashi 220
Swiss Army Knife 9
tactical knives 9, 15
Teflon 154, 220
tempering 211
Terzuola, Bob 25, 123, 126, 182
thumb disc 163, 200
thumb pin 163, 200
Timascus 89
tip down, tip up 182
titanium 88f, 119, 121, 129
tool steel 212
Torx 75
Tri-Ad lock 139

"True Stories" 11, 14
two-handed knife 195ff
utility knife 38
V-grind 106
Victorinox 11, 14
Waffenrecht 29, 38, 112, 172, 195f, 227ff
Walker, Michael 25, 118, 129
washer 154
wave 160
Wharncliffe 97
wolfram carbide 88, 216
Zytel 78

APPENDIX

KNIFE LAW

The Legal Situation in Europe

Depending on the legal situation in the countries you visit, you may find yourself in trouble if you have your practical folding knife in your pocket. For that reason, we have put together a summary of the most important points regarding folding knives. [This information makes no claim to be complete and is provided subject to change. It is current as of September 2023.]

DENMARK

In Denmark, most pocketknives are permitted, but in the case of possible criminal offenses, the authorities are very strict. You should not carry any knives at all at public events, in pubs, or in clubs, in order to avoid trouble with the police.

TOTAL BAN
- Butterfly knives
- Double-edge dagger blades
- OTFs (switchblades where you do not pull out the blade but it springs out from the front of the handle in a straight line)

BELGIUM

There is little clear legislation in Belgium, with authorities having a great deal of discretion.

MAY ONLY CARRY WITH JUSTIFIED INTEREST (legal gray areas)
- One-handed knives
- Switchblades
- Butterfly knives

TOTAL BAN
Double-edge dagger blades

Butterfly knives (or balisongs) are prohibited in many European countries.

FRANCE

Even with traditional French pocketknives, there is no legal certainty, and the authorities exercise a high level of discretion. As a rule there are no problems when the holder behaves in a socially acceptable manner.

CARRY BAN
- Lockable pocketknives

TOTAL BAN
- Blades with a length over 15 cm
- Blades with a thickness of more than 4 mm

Photo: Kershaw

LUXEMBOURG

Due to their vague definition, flippers constitute a gray area, and it's best not to carry them.

TOTAL BAN
- Butterfly knives
- Double-edge dagger blades
- Switchblades
- Assisted openers
- Blades over 9 cm long, or over 7 cm with a blade width of up to 1.4 cm

THE NETHER-LANDS

Since there are lots of prohibition zones in the Netherlands, it's best to leave pocketknives with locking systems, in particular flippers, at home in large cities, because in this regard there is no clearly defined legal situation, and they may be considered to be prohibited switchblades.

TOTAL BAN
- Butterfly knives
- Switchblades
- Assisted openers

AUSTRIA

In Austria, you only need to watch out for the specified prohibition zones where you may not carry a knife. To date, these zones can be found in Vienna, Linz, and Innsbruck.

POLAND

Everything that is not subject to a total ban may be carried in daily life. However, no knives may be carried at large events.

TOTAL BAN
- Knives with finger rings
- Double-edge dagger blades
- Knives that could possibly be weapons (according to the police's discretion)

SWITZERLAND

You have to be careful in larger cities in case there are prohibition zones. In such zones, one-handed knives may not be carried.

CARRY ONLY WITH JUSTIFIED INTEREST (legal gray area)
- Two-bladed sharpened dagger
- Switchblade
- Assisted openers

CZECH REPUBLIC

The paradise for knife enthusiasts: here there are no knife bans at all.